TWENTY-FIRST CENTURY TEACHING GUIDE FOR INDIAN SCHOOLS

SCIENCE BOOK I

Tania Ghosh is a highly experienced educator, author, and curriculum innovator with over a decade of experience teaching physics at the IBDP, IGCSE, and A Level programmes. She holds an M.Sc. in Physics and is currently a high school physics teacher at Modern High School International, Kolkata, where she also serves as an ATL team member. Tania is the founder of FutureEd Curriculum Designs, a global community for educators, and a contributor to the IB Exchange Physics Development Team. She has also served as an ATL Coordinator at Calcutta International School. A doctoral candidate in Curriculum and Instruction, she holds numerous advanced certifications from prestigious institutions such as Harvard, MIT, and Cambridge. Her mission is to empower students and educators by creating engaging, future-ready learning experiences that foster lifelong curiosity.

PEDAGOGY SERIES

Twenty-First Century

TEACHING GUIDE FOR INDIAN SCHOOLS

Science 1

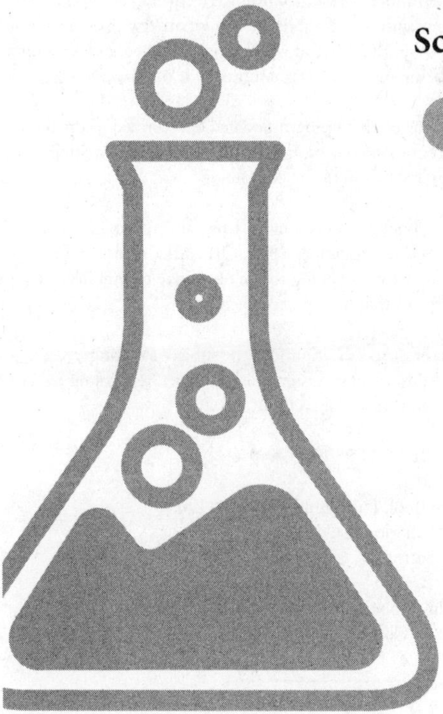

Tania Ghosh

For Classes 3–5

hachette INDIA

First published in 2025 by Hachette India
(Registered name: Hachette Book Publishing India Pvt. Ltd)
An Hachette UK company
www.hachetteindia.com

1

ISBN: 978-93-5731-440-4

Hachette Book Publishing India Pvt. Ltd
4th & 5th Floors, Corporate Centre,
Plot No. 94, Sector 44, Gurugram 122003, India

Typeset in Adobe Garamond Pro 11.5/16
by Content Respondus
New Delhi

FSC www.fsc.org
MIX
Paper | Supporting responsible forestry
FSC® C010615

Printed and bound in India
by Thomson Press India Ltd.

Contents

Preface

As a student I was never fond of examinations. It felt like a chore to me. Yet when it was interaction in the classroom or a challenge given by teachers, the love of discovering new knowledge always kept me going.

In my teaching practices I have tried to give more importance to concepts than content. The beauty of co-creating knowledge together with students has inspired me to experiment with different types of pedagogical practices.

This book began as a series of discussions of different ways of engaging students in a classroom. All my colleagues, mentors, and my educator family at FutureEd Curriculum Designs have enriched my thoughts and ideas of teaching throughout the years of my educator journey.

The NEP has outlined the ways by which teachers can focus on concepts and skills while delivering lessons. This book aids teachers with the ideas of educational theory and theorists, and bridges it with varied teaching strategies that align with it. These teaching strategies are steeped into all the skills that the NEP focuses on.

The focus has been to incorporate the topics that are mapped in the CBSE Science curriculum. This should help teachers of the national curriculum to have an understanding of how to use the book in planning classroom strategies that engage students and help the teaching learning process.

I am deeply grateful to my publishers for this opportunity that has made me delve into pedagogical practices further. The stupendous learning over the last few months was exhaustive and enriching.

Here is to more discoveries and learning! I hope you learn or relearn some aspects of varied teaching practices spelt out in the book.

Chapter 1

Behaviorism

In a school system, the foundation of teaching and learning rests on the relationship between students and teachers. In order for learning to happen, it is essential that the teacher, in some capacity, influences the behavior of a student.

An approachable teacher can easily maneuver student learning if the behavioral aspect of the students is taken care of. This entails laying down rules in the classroom, employing tactics of classroom management, providing motivational influence and understanding student psychology.

Behavioral learning theory is a branch of psychology that focuses on how people learn through their interactions with the environment.

It is often very intimidating for new teachers nowadays to step into a Gen-Z classroom, where the students have the world at their fingertips. I, as a teacher, find it very helpful to take some time out of routine teaching and just speak with students about the goings-on in their lives. Only when a rapport is built does the student respond to the teacher.

There is very little scope for Mr. Miyagi surviving in the twenty-first century, if you know what I mean.

Mr. Miyagi is the sensei of the once-bullied Daniel LaRusso, teaching him both martial arts and life lessons to protect himself. He helps shape Daniel into an honorable man, husband, and father. Mr. Miyagi's impact on Daniel and those around him was lifelong, as his teachings were wise and impactful.

Students will question, challenge, doubt, and re-question the teachers. If they do not...well, is actual teaching really happening? However, once the rapport is in place (most definitely, you cannot stop teaching until it is completely built), you lay down the rules of the classroom.

Let us now look at the concept of behaviorism:

- It is concerned with the measurable aspects of human behavior.
- It also considers how behavior changes from stimulus to responses.

Behaviorism came into the picture in the twentieth century, when introspective psychology was questioned. Introspective psychology was backed by subjective reports of mental processes and states.

Behaviorists such as John B. Watson and B.F. Skinner put forward the thought that psychology should be a science of observable and measurable events and behaviors.
They further argued that, in psychology, mental states and cognitive processes were irrelevant.
Behaviorism is not only used in the field of education but also in therapy, AI, and animal training.

The various sections of behaviorism include:
Positive reinforcement
Negative reinforcement
Punishment
Modeling
Shaping
Cueing

Positive Reinforcement: Focusing students' attention on the desired behavior. The desired behavior initially has to be verbally repeated over a period of time. Once students act on it, it is important to acknowledge it with praise. It can be in the form of a clap, a verbal acknowledgment, or a sticker or token. What you use is entirely up to you and what you think works for your students.

This serves two purposes:

- The student gains satisfaction and confidence from adhering to the norms laid down by an authoritative figure.
- The other students are motivated to do better and align with the norms.

In the science curriculum of class 3, there is a topic that introduces the idea of animals. The learning objective is:

- Animals, small and big: Which are the smallest and the biggest animals you have seen? Which have you only heard about? Which animals have tails? How many legs?
- A simple topic, definitely, but it can be approached keeping in mind behaviorism. Students may be given a small piece of paper and asked to list three names of animals in one column and their size, number of legs, whether they have tails, where they have seen them, etc.

Name of animal	Big/small	No. of legs	Tails?	Where did you see them?

Where Do We Use Behaviorism?

It is always in the instructions. The teacher may instruct the students to take three minutes to do the activity. The limitation of time will help them finish the task with focused attention. Once done, they put their hands up (waiting for their turn) and come up to pin their paper on the soft board one by one (giving everyone time to showcase their work with patience).

The teacher draws a star on the answer chits, which are left for everyone to see. The teacher also acknowledges students who have adhered to the instructions of time and have waited their turn with a double star.

The next focus of behaviorism is negative reinforcement. Well, the word negative may seem a bit off-putting, but teachers actually help students by taking away an undesirable task from the students' to-do list when they achieve a desired behavior.

This serves three purposes:

- The student wants to escape mundane/chore-like tasks and thus repeat the desirable behavior.
- It may reduce students' anxiety or stress.
- It motivates the student to repeat the desired behavior.

In the same science curriculum of class 3, we come across a topic—Shelter—which talks about homes and how we can take care of them.

Diverse discussions can be initiated by the teacher to encourage class participation. The beauty of such chapters is that students learn from their day-to-day experiences. When the teacher asks for participation, it is fluid, and everyone takes part.

Activities:

- List the ways in which your house is taken care of.
- Who helps in keeping your house clean?
- How do you contribute to keeping the house clean?

The teacher takes in all suggestions and creates a rota of duties for students who will take on the responsibility of keeping the classroom clean.

Group 1 (Week 1)	**Group 2 (Week 2)**	**Group 3 (Week 3)**	**Group 4 (Week 4)**
Parul	Sudha	Shabnam	Tina
Vimal	Hussain	Abbas	Rakhi
Gopal	Diljeet	Dhir	Mukhtar
Shekhar	Neer	Dhruv	Damon

The teacher creates a list of responsibilities/star chart:

- Cleaning the blackboard
- Putting all the chairs in place
- No litter on the floor
- All bookshelves arranged in the class library
- School bags in place
- Plant pots watered and tidied

The teacher chooses the group that has won—a group that has done their work diligently will be allowed to skip part of their summer vacation homework. Hence, you are taking away a duty/chore from those who have achieved the desired behavior.

Behaviorism also talks about when a student engages in an undesirable behavior; the age-old way of rectifying the behavior is punishment—reprimands, loss of privileges, less time at lunchtime or tiffin breaks, and extra responsibilities like setting up the auditorium to check audio/video, etc. However, the punishment should have stages of severity. A verbal warning should be followed by a diary note. If repetitive misbehaviors occur, parent(s) may be called to discuss the issue or any action that the school deems fit, as per their policy, may be taken.

Drawbacks of Punishment

In my years of teaching, I have seen that punishment often instills a fear of the teacher or fear of the subject that the teacher teaches. I remember my language teacher in primary school and how terrified we were in her classes as she tolerated no dialogue in class. Her word was the first and the last.

All of us have had an Agatha Trunchbull in our lives—a strict and authoritative figure in the brilliant children's book *Matilda*, written by Roald Dahl. Punishment should not penalize the student more than once for the same mistake. Care should be taken that all teachers do not mention the punishment to make the student(s) feel embarrassed multiple times.

There are two extremes that can happen if care is not taken in this step: the student can undergo damage to confidence or self-esteem; sometimes the student may become defiant or aggressive. In both cases, elaborate counseling and dialogue are mandatory between teacher and student, as children might not fully understand that the punishment has been devised so that the desired behavior is set in place, which will help them in the future.

In the curriculum of class 4, environmental science, there is a particular topic that requires students to think about work and play. The teacher can ask students to create a game in groups. The teacher can assign a theme or an interdisciplinary activity. Students write out the rules of the game, the duration of the game, and also the penalty for not following the rules.

The teacher should help them design behavior reflection sheets, where students reflect on their actions by filling out a form about their behavior and its consequences.

Name	What did I do wrong?	How did it affect the game?	What can I do to improve my action in this activity?

Behavior reflection sheet

This sheet is an example of how a simple consequence can serve as a punishment, where the student will not feel alienated. Instead, the student understands the undesired behavior and wants to rectify his behavior at the next opportunity.

Cueing is another process that can be considered in behaviorist theory. Here, the teacher/facilitator provides hints or prompts, which help students steer back to the desired behavior. This can be used in the completion of tasks, solving problems, and providing hints. Educators may provide cues that could be visual, verbal, or non-verbal. Pictures or gestures can also be employed in the process.

Cueing can have several benefits:

- It helps students focus their attention and memory on relevant aspects of the learning material or situation.
- It supports students' comprehension and understanding by clarifying concepts or instructions.
- It enhances students' engagement and participation by stimulating their curiosity and interest.

In the class 4 environmental science topic 'Tongue and Teeth', students are to explore the following:

- How do we taste different foods?
- How do teeth help us eat—are all teeth similar?
- Which teeth have I dropped and how are the new ones different?

In the suggested activity in the CBSE curriculum, it is said that the students may observe each other's teeth, tongue, and mouth; count teeth; and draw; experiment with different tasting items.

To successfully complete this activity, time is of the essence. Students should be given a time limit of five minutes to interact with one peer. This can be done using a *beat the clock* activity.

The teacher will set a time limit for the quick and efficient completion of the activity.

Counting each other's teeth and asking how many permanent teeth have grown:

Name of student	How many teeth in total	Calculated average number of teeth	How many permanent teeth	Calculated average number of permanent teeth

After five minutes, the teacher rings a small bell or plays music for transitions. After the bell is rung, the students move to a different peer for the same information. This will help reinforce the desired behavior and focus on the activity.

Drill and Practice

Have you ever faced this situation of working online intently and then this popped up:

Guess where you have seen it? Of course, when the internet went kaput!

On a scale of 1-10, how many of you have been obsessed with bettering your score in this dinosaur game?

Think of the features of the game. The first few seconds are easy, just testing the pace of the dinosaur as you keep pressing the key. Then come the cactus plants, first at some intervals, and then the challenge intensifies.

Here is one thing to reflect on: have you ever given up on the first try? I'm sure none of us have. Why do you think that is? The simple psychology of the adrenaline rush we get helps us overcome our limitations and accomplish something that seems doable.

Student learning should be like this—their minds should tell them that even though it is challenging, they will accomplish it with practice. So making drills and practicing something that is achievable yet challenging is what distinguishes a bored classroom from an engaged one.

I cannot begin to tell you the multifold effects this will have if you draw parallels with real-life examples.

So, when you begin teaching students about the roots of a plant, try not to start with how they look and the different types of roots. Children miss out on the connection. Why is it relevant? Why do they need to know?

Here is what you can do.

Talk to them according to their cognitive ability with reference to the following excerpt:

> Deforestation—the conversion of forested land into farms, ranches, or urban areas—has far-reaching consequences. Trees anchor the soil with their roots, and their removal leads to widespread erosion, particularly in tropical regions. Over the past decade, rapid deforestation has become a serious concern. In India, forest cover has been steadily declining for several years. Human activities such as large-scale tree felling reduce the soil's stability, increasing the risk of landslides during heavy rainfall. Roots not only reinforce the slope but also help regulate groundwater levels; without them, slope movements intensify. In hilly regions, deforestation combined with extensive construction work has contributed to frequent floods and landslides. This problem is especially severe during the monsoon season in many mountainous areas of Asia, where forest clearance has destabilized the slopes.

Based on this, we can generate a discussion on what could be the functions of a root. Some suggestions on points to discuss:

- Why do plants need roots?
- What would happen if there were no roots?
- How do plants survive?
- What key functions do the roots have to enable them to survive?

Once students are invested in the learning objective, the teacher may introduce them to the clapping game.

Teachers could use this engaging game, which involves clapping each other's hands, to incorporate drill and practice and set learning and relearning into motion.

The teacher can create phrases about the functions of roots:

1. Absorbs water
2. Prevents erosion
3. Stores food
4. Fixes nutrients
5. Holds it to the ground

So the students clap twice and say one of the phrases. They alternate between each other. The person who forgets does not get a point. This can be extended to the functions of the leaf, stem, flower, and fruit.

This reinforces knowledge in a fun way, with an eagerness to overcome challenges, just like in the dinosaur game.

Behavior Contracts

An agreement between student and teacher is referred to as a behavior contract. In the contract, the expectations of the student's behavior are outlined. The goal of the contract is challenging but attainable.

Remember when one of your family members told you: "If you get good marks, I will give you a chocolate or toy of your liking." They tapped into what you desired. Though the link to material things is not advisable, we should invest in rewarding them in kind; for example:

- Extra time in tiffin break
- Exemption from homework
- Choosing the seat you want to sit in

The forms of this behavior contract can be many. Teachers may come up with ways in which this behavior contract will be implemented. It might be in the form of a formal contract, where the teacher and students come up with the clauses of the contract. Both parties sign and promise to abide by it.

The teacher can implement a reward chart. Here, the teacher can write the names of the students in one column. The other columns would be the dates of the week or month. Every day, the students who abide by the behavior contract will receive a *start* sticker.

Stickers incentivize students to come back to it again and again and get as many stickers to show to their friends.

Behavior contracts can take the form of a weekly report that the student receives every weekend from their teacher.

How does this improve the student?

- It can improve communication between home and school.
- It can motivate the student to self-regulate.
- It can make behavior expectations crystal clear.
- It can make students more accountable for their actions.
- It can provide valuable feedback for the student.
- It can be used (and adjusted) over time.

Key takeaways:

- Be specific.
- Understand that consequence is not punishment.

Activity: Promise not to hurt the green

The CBSE curriculum in the primary section always emphasizes preserving nature. The teacher could create a very effective behavior contract with the conservation of nature in mind. Students can be asked for the reasons why we need to conserve nature, and a pact or pledge could be made from this discussion. In the school assembly, this pledge could be taken as an oath. The key points could be shown as a chart or a PPT.

In the class, the teacher could prepare a chart that features key aspects of this pledge:

- I will water the plants as per their needs.
- I will not pluck flowers from the plant.
- I will pluck fruits only when they are ready to be consumed.

The chart could look as follows:

Student name	Water the plants	Safe flowers	Safe fruits	Safe leaves
Student A	3 days out of 7	7 days out of 7	6 days out of 7	7 days out of 7
Student B				
Student C				
Student D				
Student E				
Student F				

The behavior contract should be weekly so that progression or improvement can be noticed in rogue behaviors. Allow students to sign the contract; this gives them a sense of empowerment.

Implementing Behavior Contracts:

Which is the target behavior? Focus on a behavior that is a priority and observable. Set clear expectations by holding a meeting. This enables students to have an opportunity to voice their opinions and outline the challenges they might face. This builds student agency using accountability.

Students, along with teachers, define the behavior they want to see in themselves. Students also identify rewards when expectations are met. This reward should be chosen in a way that will motivate them to abide by the contracts.

Teachers should make a plan for monitoring the way the students abide by the contract and evaluate them. Make the data visual. This will help keep track of the students who require reminders to follow the contract. Interventions are required from time to time to ensure that every student finishes the contract responsibly.

Chapter 2

Constructivism

Human beings are the most intelligent species on the planet (until the theories that AI will take over are established). But how did we manage to survive so long? Some would quote the evolutionary theory of Darwin—survival of the fittest. Have you ever wondered what 'fit' really means?

Even though Darwin was talking about biological or physiological evolution, we fail to see another kind of 'fit'. The evolution that created the immense change in us humans—our way of thinking, lifestyle, and attitude toward the world.

How did this happen? Discoveries. From fire, tools, agriculture, wheels to medicine, math, laws, phenomena and now the word of the day—AI. Were the discoveries taught to the discoverer? Most definitely not. It's the curious human nature that helps us go from point A to point B. But in order to reach B, you must have solved all the hurdles of point A.

There were discussions, arguments, banking on prior knowledge, failures, reflective thinking, and, assimilation of knowledge. Voila! We have constructivism. This is in stark contrast to the traditional approach of teaching and learning, where teachers were considered to be jars full of knowledge, filling up the empty jars of the students' minds.

In constructivism, teachers are facilitators. They help students construct their knowledge, building on the prior knowledge they already have. The students are engaged, often with their peer group, in constructing/making sense of the task at hand. While doing so, they discover the learning. Teachers who understand constructivism try to create experiences for students.

As a teacher of physics, I was sometimes crowned as an art and craft teacher. I used to have piles of papers, charts, or cardboards that facilitated students making sense of the learning. Thankfully, my school understood that a 'noisy class was an engaged class'. Students had to get out of their places to create a solid, liquid, or gaseous structure by joining hands to simulate the bonds in the molecules. Class management was challenging, but as I said, the rapport with students is all it takes.

I remember we were doing the reflection maze in one of the classes, where I brought in the school carpenter to explain angles and construction. Oh yes! People laughed. But what they did not know is that there is a method called constructivism, and it works! It really works!

Oh, and you all should read the book or watch that movie to savor this concept called constructivism: *The Boy*

Who Harnessed the Wind, written by William Kamkwamba. The buildup is surreal! Literally!

The two broad classifications of constructivism are assimilation and accommodation.

Assimilation is brand-new information fitting into an existing schema. Say a student learns that an elastic band elongates as you pull on it. As you increase the force, it snaps.

Accommodation is new information that revises and helps students relearn an existing schema. For example, a student in India sees day and night from around 6:00 am to 6:00 pm. However, when he travels, he sees that day and night times change depending on the geographical location. He accommodates and revises his concepts of day and night times.

What constructivism does:

- It engages students and creates interest as the participation of the student is in focus.
- Students engage in social interactions and learn skills of communication—waiting for their turn, respecting others, and team spirit.
- Students take the onus of constructing knowledge on their own with a little guidance from the teacher.

Difference between traditional and constructivist classrooms:

Traditional	Constructivist
Fixed curriculum valued	Students' interests valued
Repetitive learning	Building on prior knowledge
Teachers speak, students listen	Dialogue between teacher and student required
Knowledge is imparted in one direction	Knowledge construction is dynamic
Individual students work on taking notes or doing classwork	Students work in groups

Components of Constructivist Theory

- When a teacher asks, "What lights up the sky in the daytime?" they are eliciting prior knowledge.
- When the teacher asks students, "As the moon is a non-luminous object, how do we get moonlight?" they are creating cognitive dissonance, where the students are challenged by the novel problem. They relook into their schema and work on the task at hand.
- Now, the teacher may ask students to draw how the reflection of light takes place after a small group discussion. The students are given some time to discuss, and they come up to the board to draw their version

of the understanding. The teacher asks for feedback and may give his/her feedback as well. This is the application of knowledge with feedback.

- The teacher asks students to start drawing the correct diagram for the reflection of sunlight on the moon.

Constructivist Teaching Strategies

Experiential Learning

Being the youngest girl in a big family, I was always protected by my parents, relatives, and cousins. I was fairly good at studies and liked doing mathematics. The little me was proud of her grades, where addition, subtraction, and mental math were part of the testing syllabus at school. This was all on paper.

One day, there came a time when my mother asked me to go to the shop to get some household things. Since the shop was nearby, I was pretty confident. However, being 9 years old, I did not think that I had to do mental calculations with rupees and paise, that too in a few seconds. As soon as I gave the 5-rupee note, the shopkeeper said Item 1 was Rs 2.75 and Item 2 was Rs 1.75. He handed me 50 paise. I was a little zapped. During the three minutes of walking back home, I started doing the math in my mind: adding, subtracting. To my relief, the change was correct. So no scolding from my mother. That is experiential learning!

In the CBSE grade 3 EVS syllabus, there is a topic that deals with exploring children's ideas about a "plant"—plant diversity, size, where they grow, shape, color, aroma, etc.; the dependency on plants for everyday life; introduction of new plants/crops and changes observed by elders over time; plants and the climate/environment.

At the heart of this activity is learning about plants. Identification of plants comes as the first step. Teachers may show pictures of different trees in class and give students clues to identify them. Once they are sure about the learning, a walk in a botanical park with the students could be done. Students are given a handout on how to identify simple plants and trees, and they examine each tree and plant in the park and identify them.

A physical copy of a handout with pictures of trees is given to them. Students are asked to tick the plants and trees they see in the park.

Inquiry-Based Learning

The curiosity of students can be utilized in this strategy. In inquiry-based learning, a problem statement is given to the students. The students are to think and analyze to come to an explanation.

Students question certain ideas and use their curiosity to analyze the task at hand. The question posed is ideally an open-ended question. Students engage in looking at evidence, reasoning, and creative problem-solving skills.

The teacher needs to prepare for the lesson well ahead of the class. This involves thinking about the question posed to the students, how it maps into the learning objective, and what could be the guiding points for the students, etc. Understand that the teacher does not tell them the answer but helps students arrive at the answer by guiding them.

The different kinds of inquiry range from rigid and structured—confirmation inquiry—to open inquiry. Confirmation inquiry works on the fact that the beginning, the end, and the road to the end are set. Students learn how the method works through critical thinking and investigation.

Structured inquiry is when students are provided with the method of investigation and the open question. They look at evidence and reach a conclusion using their investigative skills.

Guided inquiry is when students are provided with an open-ended question, but they have the independence to design the investigation to reach a conclusion.

Open inquiry gives students the freedom to put forth original questions. Investigations happen in their own ways, which culminate in a presentation and further discussion.

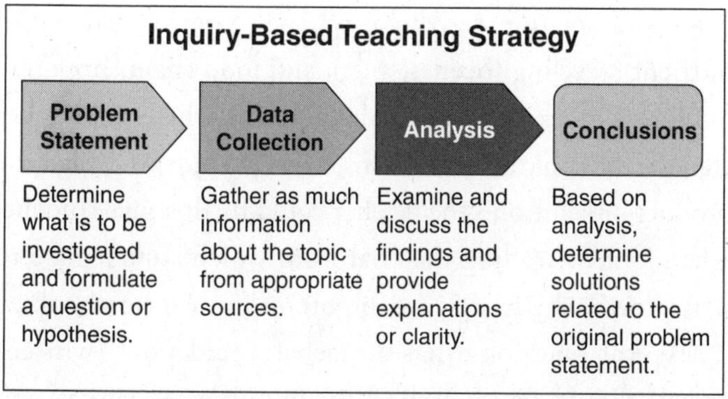

In the class 3 syllabus, this can be done with the topic that deals with exploring children's ideas of crawling animals, flyers, and insects. What different kinds of small crawling animals do you know? Where and from what do each of them hide? Which insects can crawl and also fly? Which ones bite us? Can flies make us ill? Why does a spider make a web?

An initial discussion to pique their interest could be with the questioning technique:

- What are some of the crawling animals that you see in your daily life?
- What do they eat? Where do they stay?

Problem statement: What purpose do crawling animals, flyers, and insects serve?

The students will come up with many answers, but the teacher should guide them to discuss along the lines of pollination (bees, butterflies, flies), seed dispersal (birds, ants), soil aeration (earthworms), pest control (ladybugs), nutrient recycling (beetles, ants), and food chain support.

This is an example of guided inquiry, where the teacher chooses the topic and questions, and the students design the product or solution. The teacher could further give students a handout or reading material from which students are to write down why insects are important in their notebooks.

Typical questions that a teacher could pose (written/verbal) should center around the importance, habitat, and why preserving such organisms is humane.

Student-Led Rubrics

For evaluating and grading students' work, a rubric is a very effective tool. There is a gradual buildup of the traits in a particular strand of the skill that the activity aims to evaluate. However, it is tailored to the subjects and learning objectives/skill assessments.

In our day, we had a song called "*Father Abraham had many sons…*" where, after a single verse of the song, the children funnily move their limbs and body to and fro and have to shout:

Verse

Shout: Right hand!

Verse

Shout: Right hand, left hand!

Verse

Shout: Right hand, left hand, right foot!

Verse

Shout: Right hand, left hand, right foot, left foot!

Verse

Shout: Right hand, left hand, right foot, left foot, shake your head!

Verse

Shout: Right hand, left hand, right foot, left foot, shake your head, turn around!

Verse

Shout: Right hand, left hand, right foot, left foot, shake your head, turn around, sit down!

In this fun song, the idea was to have students be alert about how to control their movements.

Students knew what was expected of them and could assess how much of the task was performed by them. No teacher had to come and give them an evaluation of their achievement.

Student-led rubrics align in the same way.

In this section, we will be focusing on giving students the independence to create a rubric.

Before you expect students to create rubrics, explicit instructions need to be provided. Teachers can create a small presentation on the topics given below. Teachers may talk about one particular topic/chapter theme and give examples of the criteria that need to be assessed.

How to develop a grading rubric

1. Select a performance/assignment to be assessed.
2. List criteria.
3. Write criteria descriptions.
4. Determine levels of performance adjectives.
5. Develop scores.
6. Write the descriptors.
7. Evaluate the rubric.

In the CBSE curriculum, there is a topic that talks about the following:

What animals eat:

- Do animals eat the same things?
- What do different animals eat?
- Do you feed the animals around you?
- What do they take from your house when not fed?
- Food of domestic and wild animals; care of domestic animals.
- Observing and listing different animals and their feeding habits.
- Discussing food given to animals.
- Observing animals being fed.
- Keeping food out and observing animals come and feed.

Ask students to write a story about seven children, each hailing from seven different continents of the world. All stories should incorporate the points mentioned above. The students are to peer-assess by creating a rubric, agreeing on the criteria mentioned in the rubric, and giving constructive feedback on how it could have been done better.

Evaluation on	1 Mark descriptor	2 Marks descriptor	3 Marks descriptor	4 Marks descriptor	Marks given by peer group
Mention of the name of the animal in the geographic region	There was a vague mention.	It was mentioned once.	It was mentioned, but the region was not very specific.	Both the animal and the region were mentioned in detail.	
Stress on the food they eat	The name of the food was not mentioned, or the food mentioned was not relevant.	Only one kind of food was mentioned.	Several foods were mentioned but not all of them are relevant.	All relevant food eaten by the animal was addressed.	
Was the animal fed? Why or why not?	It was not mentioned clearly.	It was mentioned once without details.	Details of the animal being fed were addressed, but the explanation was not given.	The story both explained whether they were fed and why/why not were they fed.	
Feeding habits	It was not mentioned in details.	Feeding habit was mentioned.	Feeding habit was mentioned with daily routine.	Feeding habit was mentioned as to what the animal ate and at which time of the day.	

If this was a rubric created by the students, how do you think it would benefit the students? Would you be able to map the rubric with the following?

1. Clarity of expectations
2. Engagement and ownership
3. Critical thinking
4. Collaboration skills
5. Self-assessment
6. Feedback skills
7. Adaptability
8. Improved outcomes

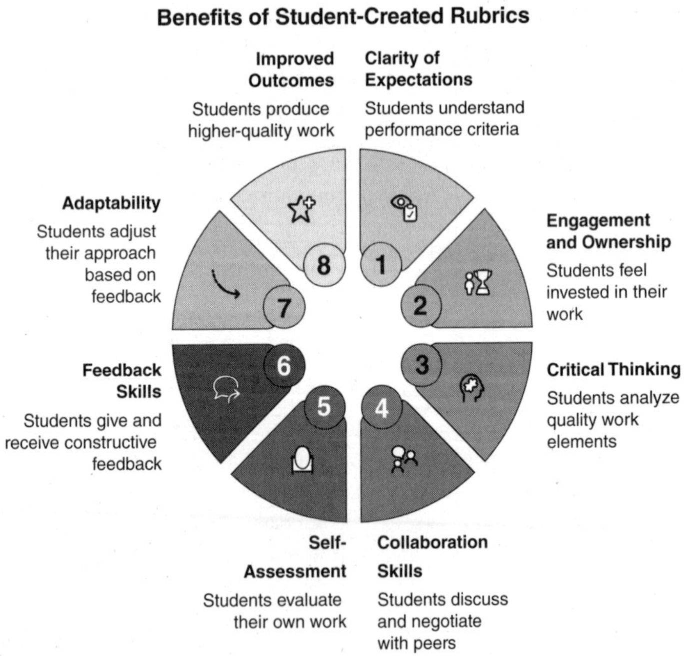

Peer-Assisted Learning

It has always been the best source of learning. Easy communication, no stringent rules, no sitting in one place and listening. It is learning from a friend. A friend who speaks your language (not the weird lingo that I hear coming up). A friend, a peer knows best how you comprehend things. So, shifting from a one-size-fits-all mentality, peer-assisted learning (PAL) is a beautiful way of information and process transfer.

Ants don't have formatted pedagogies, but ant colonies show collective decision-making skills that resemble PAL. Whether it is transporting large objects or building a nest, cooperative problem-solving and peer assistance can be seen in their activities. Such a wonderful way of exhibiting the fact that even organisms of that minuscule dimension still harness the strength of communities! We humans need to learn much from nature. The lessons that nature relentlessly teaches us get diluted in pandering to our own aspirations and egos. Well, I can go up the philosophical path, but let's stick to pedagogy!

So what works for the ants?

In some species (Temnothorax, for example), experienced members of the ant community follow rules that are laid down in their interactions. This can be compared to peer learning, and knowledge is transferred from one to another.

Pheromone trails and memory landmarks are used by ants, which are both public and private information that they work on. Some ants behave as scouts and inform the colony about new findings. Ants retain this knowledge, share it with the community, and influence the group's choice.

Memory and associative learning in ants are very responsive. They can learn, execute, and retain experiences from each other. They are naturally adaptable to conditions that are prone to change. In the peer group, they are adaptable enough to switch tasks as per the need. This is a symbol of resilient organisms.

In the EVS curriculum, parts of the plants are discussed in great detail. We look at how parts of a flower and the flower as a whole, roots and roots function as a whole, can be addressed using peer-assisted learning.

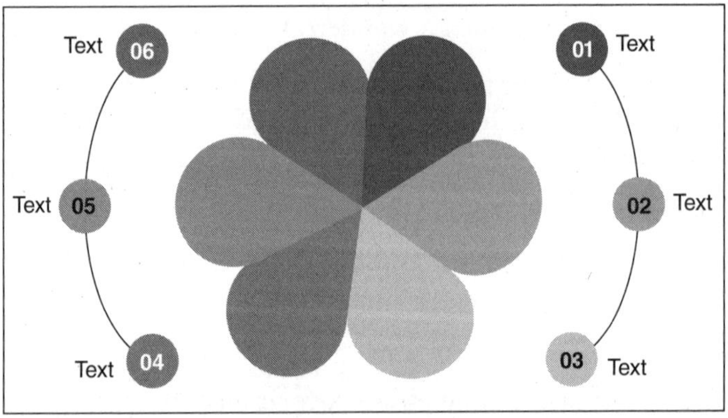

Students are paired together and are given a picture of a flower. One of the students (usually identified as the leader of the group) is given the liberty to ask questions. They are given the additional responsibility of asking a question of their choice. The text spaces in the preceding figure can be used as spaces to write answers to the questions asked.

The questions can be as follows:

1. Name the main parts of a flower.
2. Bees and butterflies are attracted to which part of the flower?
3. State the function of the sepals.
4. What are the male and female parts of the flower known as?
5. What does the flower become after pollination takes place?
6. Question of the leader's choice.

The student asking questions is told to give hints:

- Where do bees and butterflies mostly sit?
- The names start with S and P.
- The part of the plant that we eat.

Let the student come up with a set of hints themselves. This will give them autonomy and also hone cognitive abilities.

Another activity could center around the functions of a flower. The questions can be as follows:

1. Why are flowers bright and smell nice?
2. State the function of a flower.
3. Do flowers help in making new plants? How?
4. After pollination, what happens to the ovary of the flower?

Here too, the student asking questions is told to give hints:

- What do bees and butterflies do when they sit on a flower?
- Which part grows into a fruit after pollination?
- What is the need for pollen to be transferred to flowers?

Another activity could be about the process of drawing nectar and who draws it. The questions can be as follows:

1. In flowers, who collects nectar?
2. How is nectar collected by bees?
3. What is nectar used for?
4. When the bees collect nectar, what happens to the pollen?

The student asking questions can provide the following hints:

- In pictures of flowers, which insect visits it most often?
- Which part of the bees helps them collect nectar?
- Bees end up carrying something from one flower to another in the process. What is it?

This can be done with the whole class again as a formative assessment. The teacher instructs certain students to write questions on everything they have learned about roots and create a hint sheet for the others.

Scaffolded Learning

Potter, the Harry kind!

The summer I magically turned into a potter! Well, not kidding—I attended a pottery workshop, and I had to be helped. The entire process was broken down into progressive and manageable parts. Each stage had a part of prior learning woven into it.

The techniques were slab, pinch, and coil that are involved with hand-building. Then we had complex skills like slip-casting and wheel-throwing. Each of the lessons built on the previous one. We had to recap the previous class quickly before moving on with the day's work.

Competency and confidence can be easily instilled in students if they are scaffolded.

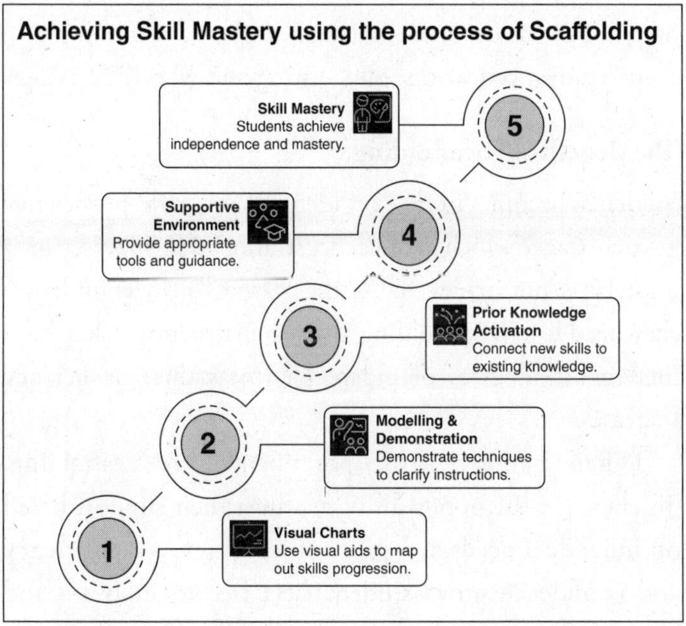

Teaching Pottery Through Scaffolding

Step 1: Introduction: Basic hand movements and clay properties.
Step 2: Pinch pots: Understand structure and form by creating simple pinch pots.
Step 3: Coil building: Create more complex shapes by learning to roll.
Step 4: Slab construction: Slabs are used to build hollow forms and flats.
Step 5: Joining techniques: For string joins, practice slipping and scoring.
Step 6: Surface decoration: Textures, glazes, and stamps.
Step 7: Advanced works: Slip-casting and wheel-throwing.

The Benefits of Scaffolding

Students become more confident. They gain proficiency at each stage, which reduces frustration that may set in if mastery is not achieved. As the learners gain confidence, they need less hand-holding and less instruction. They have incremental degrees of independence as their proficiency increases.

Differentiation gains prominence in scaffolding. Teachers get the opportunity to adjust their support based on individual needs and paces of learning. As competency and confidence grow, students feel free to innovate and create their own products.

Activity: When Birds Make Nests

The learning here would be nesting habits, materials used for building nests, and why birds choose those materials. Depending on environmental needs, students will analyze how different birds create their nests.

In the first 10 minutes, we can introduce the hook: the teacher can display different types of bird nests. Students are asked about the similarities and differences in the nests. This may include shape, color, or materials used.

The teacher can assist in drawing a comparison between houses and nests. Safety and security are highlighted. How all animals need a home, a shelter, to continue existing has to be conveyed in an empathetic way. Stress should be placed on how eggs and chicks are safe in these nests and how we should protect them.

It is imperative to share the lesson objectives with students. They will understand why and how birds build nests.

Next 15 minutes: Discussion on functions, which include raising the young, protection, and shelter.

Types: Open-cup, platform, and cavity. Give them an assignment of listing the common materials that birds use for making nests. When they come back with the list, write it down on the board. Some examples are twigs, mud, leaves, ropes, and strings.

Teachers can ask the students why birds use these materials.

Twigs help in ______.

Mud is used because ______.

Leaves would help ______.

Ropes and strings ______.

The frame of the nest is made using twigs. Mud sticks to the frame and makes the wall stronger. Leaves may help in insulation inside the nest and provide softness. This enables the bird to add structure and walls to the nest, which increases the stability of the structure.

Sweden has Treehotel, which is covered with twigs entirely. It mimics the natural nests found in the forest surrounding it. Such a place of stay is said to harness a connection between the occupant and nature.

Mud has been used to build walls in rural India for centuries. It is both traditional and sustainable. The positive aspect of this is that it is a locally sourced material. Birds too find it easy to source. Mud huts have been cost-effective, and when used with straw, they make the structure versatile and resilient.

Leaves are integrated into architecture for organic shapes and patterns.

Aesthetically, it seems to grow organically from the surroundings and looks beautiful. Ropes and strings are used for tension in a structure. Birds can create nests that are complex and look beautiful.

Sustainability, innovation, and nature's connection are discussed, highlighting how important nature can be in our existence and day-to-day living.

Group activities come next: 15 minutes.

Let's build a nest! The objective of the activity and its purpose are introduced. Teachers may ask students to bring certain items from home, such as ropes, strings, leaves, grass, glue, and cotton.

Ask the art teacher to come and help demonstrate how to layer or weave materials. Ask the participants to choose any material they want to work with.

The Guiding Steps

The steps are broken down into:

1. Which base are you going to choose? (Paper bowl/plate)
2. Choose a few layers of soft materials (cotton or grass).
3. Next, we use twigs and strings. This gives it structure.
4. Use leaves and feathers to finish off.

How Do You Scaffold?

Build the nest along with them. While doing so, narrate your actions. Talk about collaboration: How do we make the nest stronger?

Further Scaffolding

By asking open-ended questions, offering prompts, and providing feedback, we can scaffold further: questions like "What would make the nest cozier?"

Reflection will help in further exploration. Ask students whether they liked the outcome. Did they imagine the nest this way from the beginning?

They can further explore the homes of other animals and talk about similarities and differences.

Discovery Learning Experiment (Hands-On)

Indian summers in Kolkata are unbearable. With global warming, we can feel it all the more. With time, air conditioners are becoming a tool for survival. This heat is getting to us, but a small percentage of us are coping with it using technology. But can we be this selfish? What about other life forms?

One summer, we saw stray dogs, birds, cats, and quite a few animals trying to take shelter from this heat. We tried to do something for them. What could be the easiest thing? Water, of course! So some of us very smartly got water bottles and assembled them in the compound. Don't judge; we were just stepping into our teens!

Whenever we saw a dog passing by, all of us would run with a bottle of water and feed it. Soon, chaos broke out: "It was my turn to feed…" and the like. This went on for 10 minutes. Then realization dawned. We were under the sun, and our throats started drying up. So the water we had brought with us for animals and birds was consumed by us. Don't laugh!

We went from exploring concepts to manipulating the materials. We opened the bottle caps, placed them at different places in the area, and came back home. Some of us peeped from our windows to see if it was working.

Then we saw birds and dogs trying to drink from the bottles, but of course, they could not. Someone shouted, "Let's give them straws!" We glared at him, of course, but he was only trying to help! Each and every bottle was knocked down, and our purpose was defeated.

We went from bottles to plastic tumblers, and then someone got a big aluminum 'gamla'. The water in it started reaching boiling temperature, being out in the open. No one dared roam in the vicinity of the rising vapors.

So, in the end, we took heed of what the elders had to say: Get a small container of some insulated material, place it in the shade, and secure it so that it does not topple over.

Taking guidance and learning from our mistakes, we could do justice to our initial idea. We discovered and learned.

The idea of the stability of the structure and insulation was self-taught. Isn't that how learning should be? Thinking of materials, hypothesizing, discovering relationships, elders acting as guides, students taking the lead in learning and curating their own learning journeys—all of these are a part of skill-building: real-world problem-solving, interactive projects to mitigate a problem, etc. It helps in critical thinking, creative thinking, and a deeper understanding of the environment.

In the CBSE syllabus, *mapping my neighborhood* has been addressed. The students can be asked about their place of stay and what their address is. The teacher can bring a map of the city/town and ask students to circle, mark, or identify where they stay.

Students may not know this. They go back home and ask their guardians about their locality. Their guardians may help them by identifying the names of the roads they should look up on the map, landmarks, etc.

In the next lesson, they can finish identifying the place where they stay on the map.

They may identify a landmark, the name of a school, or a market that is familiar to them. They will be able to discover many friends who stay in and around their locality.

Task: They are asked to go on a stroll around the neighborhood with their guardian. They are asked to write or draw about why they think their neighborhood is unique. They need to look at all the major roads they take and the major landmarks they see on their way to school.

The conscious discovery, observations, and inferences are all weaved into this learning. Though the task is not a big one, the skills that they learn are abundant. Students get the opportunity to ask questions about their neighborhood, gather information from their guardians, collect data, observe the features of their neighborhood, make notes, and learn how to present their findings creatively. Inquiry skills and research are taken care of.

After collecting the information, they analyze it and evaluate their learning about it. In identifying their location on the map, they may encounter challenges. The beauty is how they find solutions and link what they know to what they see. Critical thinking is taken care of.

What makes your neighborhood unique? A question that is not so simple. Students think about how to express their understanding and observations. Drawings and writings require creative thinking and imagination. To convince teachers about the uniqueness needs ample power of thinking. Presentation in the form of a map, story, or PPT goes beyond the standard ways of formative assessment.

Students learn how real-world locations are mapped and can be read from maps. There is a development of spatial understanding of how the scale of these maps pans out to actual distances between places.

When they use Google Maps while traveling, they will be able to navigate. This could be given as an extension assignment, asking students to look up Google Maps or

Google Earth. Ask them to discuss one interesting aspect of each.

Students could also identify signs for hotels, restaurants, religious places, train stations, etc. in their neighborhood. They can recheck their work with digital maps to see whether their route to school and the important landmarks they have identified feature in the digital maps as well.

Even by walking around the neighborhood, students learn to understand the orientations spatially: north, south, east, and west. Students have the opportunity to practice the skill of keen observation. They learn how to take note of the importance of landmarks, roads, and places of eminence. Observations are articulated clearly when they use drawing and writing. Describing what they have seen and noted improves their cognition.

In this activity, the students have to communicate with their guardians, ask them questions, infer, and retain. This requires verbal communication and active listening. When they document their thoughts and ideas, they use writing skills to record their observations of the neighborhood.

Teamwork and collaboration are fostered when students work with their guardians and friends. They engage with the community and develop a sense of awareness and belonging to the environment.

Chatper 3

Cognitivism

Like most Indian families, I was introduced to music from a very early age. And I did not like it. Do you know why? Because it was about repetition. The teacher gave me the same *Sa Re Ga Ma Pa Dha Ni Sa* to practice. It was a chore! Every day, 5:00 to 5:30 pm, out came the harmonium and my tears.

What was the point? Well, the realization came years later. I could pick up any tune in a jiffy. Now, how do you think I did that? I processed the audio information, memorized the pitch, and used it to 'problem-solve'—my voice pitch attuned to the notes needed in the song.

Years later, I now enjoy music of all genres; Hindustani classical is still what I go back to. It's the backbone on which all musical experiences can be fleshed out.

Watch how the process of cognitivism is etched in the mind of a learner in the YouTube video.

Facilitating, leading, and providing mental routes and patterns for the student to follow. The student, Kaushiki Chakrabarty, obviously shows her innate intelligence and proficiency. She is intently using the information she has received, organized, and stored. She efficiently retrieves all that she has learned to make connections. Look at how many mistakes she is making, but she is organizing the information with every attempt.

The information is not transactional. As an individual, the student acquires and stores her knowledge, forming schemas in her long-term memory organized into categories. This experience changes the learner in the following ways:

- Information is organized strategically.
- Knowledge is stored in fundamental building blocks.
- Educators only guide the learners to effectively organize information within their memory.
- It gives the brain the ability to learn from experiences, senses, and thoughts.

The active participation of the learner is in focus. If we were to think of another analogy, it could be that of a computer, where the brain works as a computer processor. The organization of information is akin to internal coding and structuring, as in a computer.

> So, when a student knows that evaporation happens at all temperatures and that water is converted to water vapor, the teacher asks students to discuss how clothes on a clothesline dry up after some time. They think about how liquid turns to water vapor. Then they consider that there is no temperature change.
>
> They retrieve the information of where these two things fit in. It matches with evaporation. That is where the connection is made.

The Fundamental Aspects of Cognitivism

Look at the preceding image. It evokes fond memories of our childhood. What comes to your mind when you see this picture? Tintin is someone who reads, has a lot of knowledge on a variety of subjects, and can be relied upon when it comes to factual knowledge. In all, he is a learned person.

This is comprehension.

When we repeatedly see Tintin referring to books and making notes, we understand that he relies on knowledge and information. He tries to make sense of the things happening around him using logic and understanding, banking on the information he has. This gets etched into our memory.

In this picture, we see Tintin intently trying to solve a mystery. We apply our understanding of him and our inferential skills to make logical connections that only he can solve the mystery. That is how we apply our understanding.

How does cognitivism help the learner?

- Enhances learning
- Boosts confidence
- Enhances comprehension
- Improves problem-solving skills
- Helps learn new things faster
- Teaches how to form concepts

Key words and phrases needed for teachers:

- Explanations
- Demonstrations
- Examples

- Practice
- Corrective feedback
- Planning
- Goal-setting
- Organizational strategies before answering questions

Document Analysis

In the EVS curriculum of class 3, there is a chapter that deals with the beaks and claws of birds. It concentrates on the different kinds of beaks and claws, keeping in mind the need for adaptations. Students are given a printout or shown a magazine, like the one shown below:

They are asked to analyze the document. This includes students looking at new kinds of birds and their beaks and claws. The beauty of the magazine is that it shows a particular category of beaks and claws and explains the need for adaptation. Students may be asked to make a table where they write the following:

Name of the bird… Type of beak/claw… Reason for the adaptation

Enthusiastic students may be asked to draw or create the beaks and claws out of plasticine/clay. With this activity, you are working on their schema through experience and analysis.

After this is done, they can be given a worksheet where they have to retrieve the information that they organized. Here, inductive reasoning is used to answer the questions. They reason out some of the answers as they may not be explicitly taught everything they are questioned about. Here, teachers should be open about the answers and guide them to eventually come to the correct answer.

Caution: Never tell them the answers. Guide them.

They need to grow out of the concept of a question having only one correct answer.

2. Carefully observe the picture given below and answer the questions based on it.

a) Name the bird in the picture.

b) What kind of beak does the bird have?

c) Based on the type of beak, tell the kind of food this bird eats?

3. Observe the picture below and answer the question based on it.

a) What kind of beak does vulture have?

b) Compare the beak of birds in questions 2 and 3 and state the difference in kind of food habits they have.

Self-Made Case Studies

Work and play is a topic of class 3 in the EVS curriculum. Case studies are used by teachers to create interest in students. The study should be relevant to the topic at hand. The work of a teacher is to help students divide the study into manageable portions; key questions have to be identified; and relevant information gathered for research. Students should be helped to present the answers by studying the case study.

You may not have heard of a 'self-made case study'. Let's try to figure it out.

Create a chart with columns and rows as shown below.

Table 1: What do they do? Occupation chart.

Name	Father	Mother	Brother	Sister	Grand-father	Grand-mother	Uncle	Aunty
Student 1								
Student 2								
......								
......								

Table 2: What work do they do at home?

Name	Father	Mother	Brother	Sister	Grand-father	Grand-mother	Uncle	Aunty
Student 1								
Student 2								
......								
......								

Ask all students to get this information from home and ask them to fill the chart out. Give them a week to finish the charts. For classwork, ask them/give them the following questions:

Out of all listed in the chart:

- How many women work outside the home?
- How many men work outside the home?
- How many stay in your city?
- How many have moved out of your city?
- Who does the most work at home? Are they also working outside?

Students are then asked:

- How many of you want to work when you grow up?
- How many of you like a line of work that is listed in the chart?
- Why do you like it?

Students can present their understanding in their notebooks or be asked to speak about their findings.

Chunking Information

Yes! I am going to talk about Harry Potter! The sensation that it has been and continues to be. There is so much that could be planned around this phenomenon—from writing skills to business models to self-help concepts.

So rewind to the first book. After I read it, I enjoyed the discussions and debates with friends and family about how incredibly engaging the story, the movie, the characters, and the plot were.

After the initial frenzy, the mundane set in. After a few weeks, I started reading book 2, then 3, then 4… All of those stories and plots together became a bit too much sometimes. Not saying it would be the same for everyone.

I found myself looking up the previous books to recollect—the Dursleys, the Weasleys, dragons, mermaids, spells, wands… So, for people like me, when there is information overload in a short span of time, we resort to breaking it down into small manageable pieces—chunking.

What Is Chunking?

It involves grouping individual pieces of information to align with a pattern of thought clusters.

1. By grouping information, we reduce the amount of information we have to hold altogether, so that we can process and remember parts easily.
2. It reduces the cognitive load and helps assimilate topics in compartments.
3. Encoding and retrieving information becomes easy, and short- and long-term memory improves significantly.
4. Since complex information is broken up into understandable bits, chunking helps deepen comprehension of the task at hand.
5. We are not overwhelmed with a large amount of information, and effective learning takes place.

6. Students are much more engaged in the learning process.
7. It helps long-term retention.
8. Students are able to apply their knowledge in different contexts as they can efficiently retrieve chunked information.
9. It improves executive functioning skills such as planning, organization, and time management.
10. Students with learning differences have an advantage with this method as a structured approach to learning helps reduce cognitive barriers.

In CBSE, the topic of rivers and seas requires a sizable amount of cognitive load. This could be structured into 'chunks' to facilitate learning.

Chunk/Topic	Objective	Content	Activity
Introduction	Students will be able to share their prior knowledge.	—	Show maps and pictures of rivers and seas. Ask about names of rivers they know. Discuss how a river originates and where it ends.

Chunk/Topic	Objective	Content	Activity
Chunk 1: Regional changes (in the course of the river)	Students will be able to understand the changes in the geographical features of the land in the course of the river flow.	The river originates in a mountain, then flows through the plains and ends in the sea. The land flattens the nearer it is to the sea. The river slows down and becomes wider as it moves through the plains.	A video of the journey of a river may be shown. Give the students a photo/ photocopy of the course of a river and ask them to label the upper, middle, and lower courses of the river.
Chunk 2: Animals in rivers and seas.	Students will be able to identify the animals living in seas and rivers.	River animals: Fish, ducks, swans, frogs, otters, beavers, kingfishers, and herons. Sea animals: Various fish, crabs, turtles, dolphins, whales, etc.	The teacher can use visual aids like flashcards. A memory game or a matching game can be created using the flashcards.
Chunk 3: Water pollution	Students will learn about the sources and causes of water pollution.	Natural events like storms and floods. Human activities: factories, agriculture, and sewage.	Discussion: Examples of sources of pollution. The teacher can show students images of the river before and after pollution.

Chunk/Topic	Objective	Content	Activity
Chunk 4: Harmful effects of water pollution	Students will be able to appreciate the impact of water pollution on the environment, animals, and humans.	Fish and other aquatic organisms are harmed by polluted water. Polluted water causes diseases like cholera, skin rashes, and typhoid. Water becomes unsafe to be used by us, and there is a disturbance of the ecosystem.	Ask students to write a paragraph on what would happen if animals drink polluted water. They could also do the activity of JAM (Just a Minute), where they talk about the ill effects of water pollution.
Chunk 5: Protecting the rivers and seas	Students will learn about ways to prevent water pollution.	Use less pesticides and chemicals. Industrial waste should not enter rivers. Bio-fertilizer use should be increased to ensure that the rivers are clean.	Students are given the autonomy to choose how they would like to present their learning. It could range from writing a report to making a video about it.
Wrap-up (Assessment)	Students will summarize.	—	Quiz/MCQ/ worksheet/ reflection sheets.

Spaced Repetition

Tables in Mathematics

Spaced repetition is used for retaining information for a long time. This happens when you review the information at regular intervals. Students need not repeat one thing in a single session or cram information. The practice is spaced out.

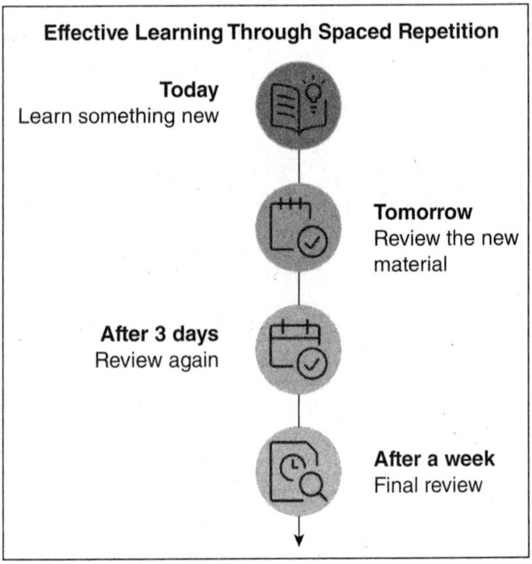

When the student or the teacher thinks that they are almost forgetting a concept, they review it together again. Long-term memory forms in this way.

The forgetting curve shows how quickly we forget new information if we don't revisit it. For students to remember a specific piece of knowledge or information, it is imperative that we give them opportunities to revisit the knowledge. Reviewing information will do the following:

- Help reinforce information in memory.
- Reduce the frequency of reviews over time.
- Help in long-term memory retention.

Do you remember your 7 times multiplication tables?

Think back on how we were trained to remember and recall the multiplication tables. It was spaced repetition.

It started with writing the tables down. It came back with mental math, then with using multiplication tables with problem sums, and then with fractions, decimals, the unitary method, and division. Now, it has become second nature. You have it imprinted in your head. 7 times 8 equals 56 is as easy as saying what your name is. (It is okay if you take a bit of time!)

How can you include this type of practice in a more innovative way?

Chanting, flashcards, skip counting, fill in the blanks, matching games, timed quizzes, bingo, group recitation, puzzle cards, memory race, and mixed quizzes.

Task Types

Learning for the first time, practice and quick recall, mixed practice, speed drill, and quiz/assessment.

What are some techniques that support repetition? Chunking, songs/rhymes, color codes, anchor facts, etc.

Reinforcement

We can use card sorting, peer challenge, clap and speak, roll the dice, and climb up and down the stairs.

In the CBSE curriculum, the theme of *paying for travel* covers currency, coins, symbols, and language. Thus, an integration of language and math becomes a possibility. The discipline of social studies also comes into the picture—how different countries have different currencies, how they are related to each other, etc. Conversion of currencies can also be taught, as well as why certain currencies are accepted in most countries.

So what are the key factors that you want students to retain?

- Coins, notes, and currencies
- The national symbols on money for different countries
- The language that appears on the paper used for money
- When do you use it—while traveling, buying tickets, buying food, buying merchandise

The goal is to help students be confident in identifying, using, and understanding real-life travel situations.

What Would the Plan Look Like?

Week 1: Introduction to currency: Coins and notes: Sorting and matching flashcard activity that helps with visual memory and tactile practice.

Week 2: The important symbols on money (Ashoka Pillar, Mahatma Gandhi). Students could be given a black-and-white outline of a currency note and asked to label and color it by looking at a picture. Visual recall and storytelling would work at this juncture.

Week 3: Languages on currencies: Students learn and discover languages—Bengali, Hindi, Tamil, etc. This would help them spot scripts of Indian languages and understand the idea of unity in diversity—how every language and culture makes up India.

Week 4: Using the knowledge of the real world: Ask the children to create short scripts and enact real-life situations, for instance, helping a foreigner who is visiting India. Ask them to include humane qualities like empathy and acceptance. They may include situations like buying tickets, helping them pay bills, etc.

They might need more than a lesson to showcase the plays. Help them arrange chairs, tables, and other props if possible.

Day-Wise Break-Up

1st day: Introduction and usage of visuals (notes/coins)
2nd day: Matching activity (recall)
4th day: Worksheet that uses memory
7th day: Roleplay
14th day: Reflection focusing on concept gaps
21st day: Peer questioning

Activities that might boost memory:

- Which is real and which is fake? Students identify the characteristics of real currency and differentiate it from counterfeit notes.
- Using the information given below, make a game called *currency detectives*, where they would play against one another and act as detectives.
- The students could be asked to write out the language scripts on the note or count the number of languages written on the note.
- The students could play currency bingo with images of currencies around the world.

How to Spot Fake Indian Currency Notes

1. Gandhiji's Watermark

The portrait of Mahatma Gandhi on every rupee note is more than a tribute—it's a key security feature.

- A genuine note has a faint but clear watermark of Gandhiji's face along with the denomination (e.g., '100' on a ₹100 note).
- Counterfeit notes often have blurry, rough, or greasy watermarks made with heavy oils, lacking clarity. How to check: Hold the note against a light source. If the watermark is clear and consistent, the note is likely genuine. If it's faint, unclear, or missing, it may be fake.

2. Number Formatting

The numbering on a genuine rupee note follows strict consistency:

- Even spacing between numbers
- Same size, font, and perfect alignment

Warning signs: Uneven spacing, mismatched sizes, or inverted/misaligned numbers can indicate a counterfeit.

3. Ink Quality

Genuine notes use crisp, sharp printing for all text, borders, and images.

- Colors should be vivid, and lines unbroken.
- Fakes may show dull ink, greasy texture, faded areas, or broken lines.

How to check: Hold the note under good lighting and inspect the print quality closely.

4. Security Thread

A genuine note contains an embedded security thread running through the paper, not just printed on top.

- When held up to light, you should see the text 'Bharat' (भारत) in Devanagari and the note's denomination clearly on the thread.

Warning signs: Threads that appear printed, vertical, or only on the surface are signs of a fake.

5. Micro-Lettering

Real currency features micro-lettering—tiny printed text that's clear under magnification.

- Found near Gandhiji's portrait and around 'Reserve Bank of India'.
- Genuine micro-text is sharp and continuous. Counterfeits often have blurred, inconsistent, or missing letters.

How to check: Use a magnifying glass to confirm clarity.

This could further be extended to cross-curricular themes—the calculation of currency addressed along with mathematics. The symbols on the currency notes would be EVS. The scripts on the notes would represent languages.

In the end, let them create and design their own currency note and explain what they have included.

Social Reconstruction

In the month of January, we celebrate **National Road Safety** week. During the week—11 to 17 January—we see a lot of students standing outside schools with awareness campaign placards, such as 'No horns please' and, 'Let us obey the traffic rules'. Many people encourage them for their spirit.

The sad part of this is that this happens just once a year. This should be a year-round activity, maybe not with the intensity shown during Road Safety Week itself but with a continuity of sorts.

Education is an effective tool that could be used to address social issues, promote social justice, and evoke critical consciousness. Teachers are thought to be agents of social change. The focus is on social injustice and critical awareness. The students are given a chance to critically analyze social issues that will empower them to drive change.

With a gamut of problems looming in the future, there is a requirement for students to know which pressing topics they should be concerned about. Some generic examples are given below for teachers to understand the theme and essence of this method of teaching.

- Investigate problems in society, like climate change and pollution. They may analyze local environmental data and come up with sustainable solutions.
- The quality of water in their locality may be tested. They can also conduct a study on ecosystems as part of experiential experiments. They can keenly observe the disparities in health and the environment.
- Ethical dilemmas, like genetic engineering and AI, form a part of higher-order discussion. Technological advancements and their social impacts can be key areas of discussion.
- During the pandemic, we saw our whole community come together to assist one another. The pandemic response teams were of considerable significance in those trying times. Students can work on roleplay where they reflect on what actions were taken by these teams,

planning and policies focused on, etc. Similarly, they can organize a climate summit and explore the interplay between science, play, and policy.

- Service learning initiatives may also be considered where community-engaged projects are undertaken. A simple example would be public health awareness campaigns.

Though this kind of teaching strategy seems engaging and holistically enriching, there are some challenges.

At the end of the year, students are not tested explicitly on the skills they picked up in the activities concerning this topic. Students are tested on what they remember and apply. Standardized testing does not help in differentiated learning.

In certain school settings, there may be a culture of perception of bias. Moreover, there might be other social influences where the indoctrination of concepts may settle into the students' minds. Care should be taken to strategically introduce the idea of questioning biases and to make students open-minded enough to accept each other's opinions.

We have seen discoveries in the past that meddled with the status quo of the era and created a lot of upheaval. So care should be taken to adopt strategies that incorporate the idea of debating the status quo.

Moreover, resource limitations, lack of teacher training, and resistance to curriculum changes jeopardize the idea of social reconstruction.

In primary school, there can be many opportunities for social reconstruction.

In the CBSE curriculum of EVS, the topic on family and friends deals with sensitivity to the elderly and physically challenged. The topic very beautifully addresses our senses and how privileged we are to have them. The teacher has to pave the way to the humane quality of empathy. How would someone feel if they were deprived of one sense in their life? It is imperative to teach students how to treat others with kindness and not to differentiate against them for their misfortunes.

Students should be spoken to about illustrious characters like Stephen Hawking, the brilliant scientist who was able to give us ground breaking theories in physics even while suffering from a serious disease.

Stephen Hawking

Students can be asked to plan for roleplay where they would show how being kind makes everyone happy or why it is necessary to be kind to all people, no matter who they are and what drawbacks they have. They may be given a roadmap of how to plan the roleplaying, including different roles to be assigned to each student in the group and a timeline until the execution of the task.

Responsibility	**What to do**	**Name of the student**
Leader	Assigns roles to group members Keeps track of the progress	
Scriptwriter	Writes the dialogues Explains the plot to the actors	
Actors	Practice and execute the play	
Director	Helps with the expressions and pitch of the voice	
Narrator	Narrates parts of the play Introduces the play and characters	

Timeline

Day 1: Assign roles and tasks.

Day 2: Scriptwriter sits with the group to plan the play.

Day 3: Scriptwriter gives dialogues to the actors and a rehearsal is done.

Day 4: The director refines the expressions and voice modulation of the actors.

Day 5: Final rehearsal.

Day 6: Execution of the play.

In the CBSE curriculum, among other topics, there is one topic that is very close to my heart. It deals with child labor. I remember, when I was young, there was a boy who worked at a tea shop in my locality. He was one of seven children and the only boy among six sisters. His name was Poltu, or so I remember. Being younger than me, my cousins and I used to give him candies and samosas when we had extras to spare (we were not very selfless). Poltu, during his teenage years, turned to addiction, and some years later, he was nowhere to be found. Education could have changed his entire life path.

Students in primary school should be made to appreciate that there are children who are deprived of a childhood due to their poor economic conditions. They can be asked to make a gratitude poster and take a pledge to spread awareness about the illegality of child labor in their neighborhood.

I am grateful because ____________________________

____

Signature: _________________________________

I pledge to ________________________________

____

Signature: _________________________________

In this topic, there could be a visit from a social worker who talks about the repercussions of child labor—how it affects children and society at large. This has to be carefully curated for young learners. The teacher needs to speak to the visitor to appraise them of the level of understanding of the students.

Society as a whole rests on the work of many individuals who are never highlighted. Without these people, our society would not progress smoothly. These people are our helpers and help society function well.

In the CBSE curriculum, there is a topic that looks at how they learned their skills. This covers community helpers like cobblers, gardeners, tailors, drivers, and many more. Students nowadays might take such helpers for granted. Only their parents know the kind of 'heart attack' they have when these arrangements don't work out! I am sure many others will vouch for the fact that a working woman in India is quite dependent on these societal helpers.

To get students to appreciate them, a community-engaged project can be planned. The school gardener, canteen cook, school uniform tailor, school bus driver, etc. can be invited to the class for an informal interaction with the students.

They can be asked the following:

- Their names
- Where they come from
- How much time it takes for their commute to the workplace
- When they start and their daily routine
- How many family members they have
- At what age they started working
- If they had an option, which occupation they would choose

Students are asked to take down notes and make an infographic to celebrate the people who help us. They are requested to thank them for their work and always be cordial toward anyone who helps us lead a good life.

Another very pertinent topic is waste disposal. A sustainable way of utilizing garbage is composting, which is gaining popularity as it is easy and eco-friendly.

What Is Compost?

Compost is made by decomposing organic waste like dry leaves and fruit and vegetable peels and scraps. It improves soil quality and works as a natural fertilizer. It can be used to enhance plant quality.

Students can try making compost with their teachers and take the help of the school gardener to utilize it in school. There are many benefits of composting as it is environmentally friendly and reduces kitchen waste.

Students can create a step-by-step guide and present it to students in another class. They must advertise and recommend the benefits of composting. They could create a pamphlet or flyer and distribute it to other students as a handout.

Critical Pedagogy

On October 26, the long stretches of St. Bartholomew Beach in Poovar will host a large-scale clean-up drive. The event is being organized by the Ocean Students Community in partnership with STENUM-Asia, with the goal of preserving coastlines and raising awareness about protecting marine ecosystems.

Founded in 2020, the Ocean Students Community is based in coastal areas from Adimalathura to Pozhiyoor. The group focuses on uplifting coastal communities and safeguarding the oceans. Its members are primarily children of fishermen and others closely connected to the fishing industry.

In the above paragraph, a clean-up drive is covered, which happened in the month of October 2024 at Bartholomew Beach in Poovar. Participants were from the Ocean Students Community. They worked with NSS volunteers from a nearby school. The participants have been doing this since 2020.

This sort of activity has social relevance. When this type of activity is absorbed into the larger curriculum, education then addresses social issues, promotes social justice, and works on the critical consciousness of students.

Why would we want that? We want to build global citizens in our classrooms—who question and strive to improve the status quo if needed. Teachers are regarded as agents of change, facilitating the process along the way. The focus is always on social justice and critical awareness.

A burning example of a student who worked for a cause (critical pedagogy): Swedish schoolgirl Greta Thunberg turned a lot of heads as she raised awareness about climate change. Greta was born in Stockholm in 2003. She first learned about climate change when she was eight. Greta started suffering from depression when she was 11 or 12.

At the same time, she was diagnosed with Asperger's Syndrome, a form of autism.

Greta has been able to raise a lot of awareness among young people, even though she has not devised any specific environmental strategies.

In the year 2019, in the month of March, climate campaigners across the world coordinated the first-ever global strike for climate—1.6 million campaigners from 125 countries.

Since then, many global campaigns for climate action have been undertaken. Politicians and policy makers have taken notice of this movement.

She's given rousing speeches to politicians, to the EU parliament, the UK parliament, to protesters, and more. She's appeared in documentaries and has had loads of books and articles written about her. She's even been nominated for a Nobel Peace Prize!

Do you remember 'Go as you like'? We always looked forward to that day when we could wear fancy clothes and have a 'study-free' day. We can give it a deliberate twist to tune it to critical pedagogy. Let's call it a special day for special ones!

In the EVS CBSE curriculum of class 3, the chapter on family and friends covers the elderly and physically challenged individuals. It is a brilliant opportunity to teach children about our responsibility as citizens and about empathy.

Roleplaying: Students may be given chits to choose which role they are going to play—an elderly person or a physically challenged person.

ELDERLY PERSON

PHYSICALLY CHALLENGED

Students have to plan one unique problem that elderly or physically challenged people face. Here, they need to reflect on the daily trials and tribulations of these individuals. Once they go through it, they will be thinking critically and using creative ideas.

One by one, they come and state in one sentence what problems physically and emotionally challenged people go through. This activity would most definitely evoke empathy in all students. They can think of how they can alleviate the pain and problems, hence bringing about a change in society.

Teaching through roleplaying involves several key steps:

- The teacher has to establish clear learning objectives for the roleplaying exercise.
- The teacher selects a relevant scenario and defines the characters or roles that students will take on.
- Teachers will have to help students prepare their roles. They may inform them of detailed instructions and role documents.
- If needed, a detailed explanation of the situation, roles, and setting is to be given.
- Students need to be allowed to plan their roles and be given time to do so.
- Students perform their roles while other students note some striking roleplays.

- Discussion of the roleplay—how realistic was it? Which act was surprising? How could it be done differently? What were the key takeaways?
- Assessment: Teachers have to evaluate student performance and learning outcomes.

Community-Engaged Projects

When I travel for my daily needs and occupation, I see two very distinct differences from my childhood times. One is that there are so many more private cars plying the roads than before. The second is that all the people in public places are glued to their screens.

This affects us as a community. I used to know all the faces on the bus I took to school. I spoke to many uncles and aunties who traveled the same route for their daily activities. I knew what was happening in their families as they engaged in discussions in that little community of the public bus. We used to get worried if a known face did not take the bus for a couple of days.

And now, the sense of community has changed. Though not much can be done as this change is natural due to technological advances, we can try to include a sense of appreciation for the people who help in our community. Students nowadays don't get to interact much with their near and dear ones, so the lives of people out of their immediate family are quite difficult to be understood by them.

The CBSE curriculum gives a topic in class 4 science—how they learned their skill.

Could you think of ways to get this to be part of a community project?

Here is a way how: Ask students to seek out people in the community who help them live comfortably and ask them about their skills:

- People who mend shoes
- People who maintain the garden
- People who bring milk for them every day
- People who drive their school buses/cars
- People who repair their cars
- People who stitch their clothes

Though this could be done over a week, teachers could initiate this activity by inviting the cook of the school canteen, the gardener of the school, the school bus driver, the cleaners of the school, and whoever helps out at school. They should be introduced with their full names, and they should be seated at different places in the class. Students should go to them in turns to learn about them.

They can be given a questionnaire:

Community Helper Skills Questionnaire

1. What is your job?

 ____

2. What specific skills do you use?

 ____

3. How did you learn these skills?

 ____

4. Who taught you the most important skills for your job?

 ____

5. Do you practice or improve your skills regularly?

 ____

6. Have you taken any courses?

 ____

7. What new skills have you learned since you started your job?

 ____

8. What changes have you noticed in your job since you started?

 ____

This could be continued for a week, where they talk to people in their community and gather this information. They could then display it as a poster with pictures of their community helpers and celebrate their work.

Teachers should point out why it is essential to treat every job equally and what would happen if we did not have these skilled people in our community.

Emergency Plan for the Community

NDMA Vision

The National Disaster Management Authority envisions building a safer and disaster-resilient India by adopting a holistic, proactive, technology-driven, and sustainable development strategy. This vision seeks to involve all stakeholders and foster a strong culture of prevention, preparedness, and mitigation across the nation.

Functions and Responsibilities

As the country's apex body for disaster management, NDMA is entrusted with formulating national policies, plans, and guidelines to ensure timely and effective responses to disasters. It develops and approves the National Plan, as well as disaster management plans prepared by central ministries and departments, ensuring they align with national objectives. NDMA also issues guidelines for states to prepare their State Plans and directs ministries to integrate disaster prevention and mitigation strategies into their development program. Its role extends to coordinating the implementation and enforcement of these policies, recommending funding for mitigation efforts, and providing assistance to other nations affected by major disasters when required. In addition, NDMA undertakes measures for disaster prevention, preparedness, mitigation, and capacity building, while also framing broad policies and guidelines for the functioning of the National Institute of Disaster Management.

The NDMA is an able unit of the government of India that works dedicatedly to mitigate any inconvenience caused by natural and manmade disasters. It is also part of the SENDAI framework and works tirelessly to help outside of India as well. India has also donated vaccines to countries that needed them during the pandemic.

But why are we talking about this? The awareness of times of disaster and how to deal with crises is the focus of the next activity.

In the curriculum of science in CBSE for class 5, there is a topic called Shelter—What do we do in times of emergency? Let's be ready—floods/earthquakes/cyclones/fire/storm/lightning.

Making an emergency plan: Students are given an activity to make a poster about

The key factors to be considered in this activity will be safety and preparedness during emergencies. Some hints are given below:

1. Risk assessment
2. Emergency contact information

3. Communication plan
4. Evacuation routes and shelters
5. Emergency supplies
6. Plan for pets
7. Home safety measures
8. Training and drills
9. Documentation and insurance
10. Local resources and alerts
11. Special needs considerations
12. Community involvement

Community Guest Speakers

Do you know who this is? Most people don't. If you do, you are welcome for tea and hours of discussion on his philosophy.

J. Krishnamurti (1895-1986) was one of the greatest thinkers. He had a huge following worldwide. He spoke to large audiences and spent a lot of time debating and discussing his ideas with writers, educators, philosophers, and scientists. He was keen on the need for a radical change in the thoughts of mankind.

At the heart of his teaching was:

Truth is a pathless land. Man cannot come to it through any organization, through any creed, through any dogma, priest, or ritual, nor through any philosophic knowledge or psychological technique. He has to find it through the mirror of relationship, through the understanding of the contents of his own mind, through observation and not through intellectual analysis or introspective dissection.

It is safe to say that I am a fan, perfectly aligned with his free thoughts of man being capable of charting his path through experiences. Krishnamurti did not advocate any religion or country. He did not belong to any rigid ideology or political school of thought. He was a visionary to ask people to discard these ideas that divide us and bring in conflict and war. He reminded us that we are human beings first and he insisted on the philosophy of reflecting on human experiences.

His ideas are timeless and relevant in all settings. Manmade beliefs were not his cup of tea. He did not talk about nationalistic sentiments or believe in sectarianism but spoke about giving direction to life. He spoke like a friend, not with tradition-based knowledge but from his own insights into the mind of humans. People found his words refreshing and easy to relate to.

In CBSE, there is a topic of water in our lives. Here, activities that you do using water are discussed in detail. Cultural expressions about water, rains, and rivers are discussed in detail. Bringing in a community guest speaker will have a lasting effect on students.

The importance of water can be integrated with the help of a community speaker, who could be an environmentalist, an NGO representative, or a public figure.

Ask them to talk to the children by relating how easy or difficult it is to have water at their disposal. They can talk about how water has been central to us, our civilization, and our prosperity. They can discuss Mesopotamia around 2500 BCE, the intricate irrigation system, and rivers being the mode of transport. They can explain how trade flourished and people lived in a civilization that helped them become better individuals.

Industrial Revolution: Victorian Era

Water was central to the Industrial Revolution. It was the primary source of power and sanitation. The water wheel was the main source of power for factories, while transportation was through canals that helped move materials and goods. But man wanted more, so we began using and abusing something that gave us so much. The disposal of waste started in our pristine waters. Then there was a rise in steam power, and water pollution began here.

Iraq: Water Crisis

Declining river flow, climate change impacts, and infrastructure deficiencies have led to severe effects on agriculture, livelihoods, and public health systems. Decades of conflict have given rise to concerns over the equitable distribution of resources.

Across time and cultures, water has been a universal connector. Teachers can print or give this paragraph to the students to read:

A Water Droplet's Journey

Imagine you are about to embark on a journey. Close your eyes and picture yourself as a tiny water droplet.

It's a cold winter day in Glacier Bay National Park, Alaska. You drift high above the earth, suspended in a cloud among countless other droplets. The air around you is icy, and the cloud feels still yet alive with motion.

A powerful, frigid wind sweeps past, nudging and spinning you. Dust particles swirl into your cloud, and you bump into your neighbors as the air grows colder. Slowly, your outer surface begins to freeze. Tiny arms of feathery ice crystals start forming, growing longer and more intricate. You have become a snowflake—unique, beautiful, and unlike any other. Heavier now, you can no longer float, and gravity gently pulls you from the cloud. Around you, thousands of other snowflakes fall in a silent white descent.

You land high on a mountain, in a rocky hollow called a cirque. Snow continues to pile on top of you, pressing you down. Your delicate arms change shape under the weight, becoming smoother and rounder. The air grows thin as more snow compresses around you.

Beside you, water trickles down and freezes, binding you to the snow and ice around you. Shapes merge until you are part of a much larger ice mass—solid, heavy, and cold. Time slows, and the world becomes still as you lie deep within the darkness of the glacier, waiting for the next step in your long journey.

The write-up talks about a water droplet transforming into a snowflake in Glacier Bay and becoming a part of it. When the glacier cracks, the droplet falls into the ocean. It is part of an iceberg now. This could encourage students to think and reflect on nature and help them with creative ideas.

Inclusive Classroom Jobs

I grew up in a Christian missionary school. The strict discipline has made me who I am. The sisters and teachers guided us through value education classes, where we had the liberty to talk and reflect on what mattered to us. The teacher would clarify our doubts about what we felt and what we were going through.

Their idea of inclusive classroom jobs helped us be accountable and responsible in our work and in our lives. We were divided into four houses. Each of the houses had turns to take one responsibility per fortnight.

One week, it was the duty of House 1 to make charts for the classroom softboards. House 2 was on lunchroom duty, where they took care of the discipline when students were having lunch. House 3 was on after-school clean-up of the classrooms. House 4 had uniform and general discipline.

We were a mixed group of people, loving one responsibility and disliking another. I remember I could not wait to make charts. I disliked reminding people about the code of conduct and disciplining them (something I have to do now).

Staying back was a pain. We had to wait until everyone left and then put the chairs up, inverted, on the table so that helpers could sweep the floors easily. We picked up any stray paper on the floor and put it in the bin. We switched off the lights and fans. This irritated us for sure, but later, we understood—it built character by being responsible for the community and fostering empathy while helping each other.

The theme of big and small animals can be addressed using the strategy of 'inclusive classroom' in EVS of the CBSE curriculum. The inclusive classroom jobs in the early years or primary years can be assigned with a lot of thought. Teachers may design the roles of the students around this theme. This will ensure that every child is invested in the task and will improve student engagement.

A detailed idea of inclusive classroom jobs is given below:

1. **The Storyteller (About Animals):** This person is responsible for letting their friends know about animals through a short story, rhyme, or poem in their circle time or in literacy lessons. They may sing using certain keywords, use sign language to explain an aspect of the animal, narrate a story with charts and visuals, etc. The communication style that is convenient for the children must be kept in mind. Some may speak, others may indicate it in a diagram while speaking, partner with a peer, and take turns to talk about the task. There are many modes in which this task may be addressed, and it encourages students to participate actively. They use this opportunity to communicate. The whole class gets ready to listen to what their friends have to say and uses active engagement to understand. They also develop narrative skills.
2. **Chart In-Charge:** Tactile leadership for a visual treat! Managing resources in the classroom is a huge responsibility. Making others bring in or make a chart requires consistent effort on the part of the leader. They may ask students to decorate the class softboard with an activity. They tell each student to bring cutouts of animals.

Once they do, these students ask the teacher for Velcro. With the help of their friends, they attach the Velcro to the pictures, which are then attached to the softboard. Fine motor challenges are overcome—attaching, presenting, and organizing the board. Moreover, they could do a comparison chart of big and small animals. It allows students with a knack for visual work to shine. The leader also learns organizational skills through this activity.

3. **Which Size Goes Where?** A student is given the responsibility to sort pictures, toys, or cutouts into two categories—big and small. This hands-on sorting activity helps develop motor skills. They can point toward the pictures to categorize them, place them physically on a sheet to sort, or keep them in two containers. Even if they do not want to use their verbal skills, they are able to denote each of the animals using their mathematical understanding of sizes.
4. **Roleplay: Zookeeper:** In their world of drama, there could be a zookeeper who takes care of the toy animals. They can bring in fake food for the toy animals and enact it in front of their friends. They can explain in detail the nature of the animals. They could make imaginary sheds/homes and explain the activities of the animals—where they sleep, when they sleep, etc. Students like to be involved in mimicking real life, and this engages them. They can use their imaginations and narrate anecdotes in their dialogue while in the play.

This generates fun in an inclusive way.

A student who may not be able to answer questions in written form to express his learning can be assessed in this way. This also fosters empathy for people whose jobs are not very flashy—people who help the community and work behind the scenes.

5. **Lead the Music:** This student assists the teacher in selecting a class song and leading it. The song chosen should be related to a love for animals. They can use nursery rhymes to make the class fun and engaging. This student may choose actions like clapping, snapping, or jumping to emulate the action required to describe the animal or just to enjoy the rhythm. This rhythm, along with sound or movement, builds coordination among peers and helps improve people skills. Overall, it builds the confidence of the student in focus.
6. **Let's Pair Up:** Pairs of students group together and look for books that focus on the various aspects of animals. The stories should focus on habitats, babies, sizes, and food of these animals. Children can use a large variety of literacy levels to express, read, and support each other. Differentiation can be ensured this way. One child may read the book, and another may look at pictures and explain how they relate to each other. They may make small notes in their notebooks and write down the phrases or sentences on how each of them relates to the animal's behavior, food habits, habitat, and size.

Chapter 4

Idealism

Who do you want to be when you grow up? Haven't we heard this question before?

I wanted to be like my teacher. If we go into the psyche of children, they idolize people whom they believe to be ideals. When I asked a child why he wants to be Sachin Tendulkar, he said, "He can play every shot. He is always smiling and is perfect when he is batting."

Honestly speaking, in the world of glitz and glamour, Sachin Tendulkar can be given the title of an ideal sportsperson. He showcases focus, moral character, intellect, and being grounded.

The core beliefs of idealism start with the mind. The constructs of ideas are fundamental reality rather than being present in the physical world from the onset.

It's like Mark Zuckerberg wearing the gray T-shirt, with no glitz and glamour but cultivating critical thinking, creativity, and a love for learning.

The emphasis is on the development of moral character, mind, and spirit over material or practical skills. The teacher's role is to be a moral example and guide. They are to shape students' character and intellectual development.

The educational aims of idealism are intellectual growth, moral development, spiritual understanding, and self-discipline.

Planning a Socratic Dialogue

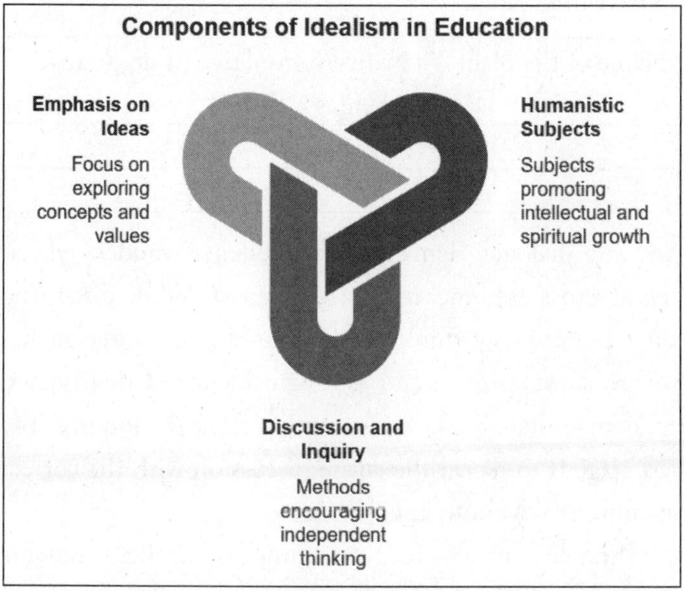

Lesson for class 3: *Should We Grow Plants from Other Regions in Our Locality?*

Socratic dialogue is used to encourage students to be critical thinkers and pique their curiosity. This lesson will explore the concept of growing plants from other regions of the world. It will give students an understanding of native and non-native plants and their importance. Students can also practice their communication skills by engaging in dialogue through open-minded questions.

In the procedure, the teacher could show images of native and non-native plants of the region. For non-native plants, a map could be shown indicating where they are said to have originated.

Name of the plant	Native/non-native (if non-native, where is it from?)

Socratic dialogue demands that students wonder, reflect, refine, cross-examine, restate, and repeat. While discussing their points, they think about what the other person has to say, summarize it, and ask for evidence of their views. Students restate the new assumption from the inquiry. The last stage is to repeat the entire discussion with the correct assumptions without any fallacies.

These lead to new ideas and innovations, help students reach a consensus, foster people and cultural understanding, resolve conflict, and help build communication skills.

The focus of this activity is how native plants help biodiversity and are adapted to their local environment, whereas non-native plants mostly require more resources and can harm the natural ecosystems. They will cover the benefits and ethical dilemmas that need to be looked into (qualitatively).

The teacher can help with the following opening questions:

- What kind of plants do you see in your locality? Name them.
- Who do you think brought them here?

Core questions:

- What would happen if other non-native plants are grown in our locality? Is there a need to grow them?
- Students will think about water needs, pests, fertilizer needs, etc.
- Let them think about how this could affect other organisms—birds and insects. What would happen if too many non-native plants were grown? (The idea of invasive plants and biodiversity may be introduced here.)

Questions on critical thinking:

- Why do farmers in a region only grow a certain type of crop?
- Why don't they try new ones every season? How can that help us?

What would they learn from this activity?

Apart from recognizing the benefits and limitations of native and non-native plants, students develop skills of reasoning by weighing pros and cons and respect for each other during the discussion.

Emphasis on Humanities
Leaf-Print Craft on Earth Day
Types and Parts of a Leaf

This activity would help students understand and appreciate nature, creativity, and aesthetic expression while connecting it to the humanities and celebrating Earth Day. The teacher may start with the idea of why we celebrate Earth Day. The scientific significance of the day should be discussed. Discuss how we have celebrated nature and human connection historically.

The Leaf-Printing Activity

Materials required:

- Flat dry leaves (dried and pressed)
- Paints (bright colors—orange, red, yellow, green)
- Paintbrushes
- Palettes
- Folded newspapers that can act as the canvas for leaf printing
- Napkins/towels
- Apron

Collecting leaves: Teachers can organize a walk in the garden where students can collect dry leaves of every shape and size. The teacher collects all the leaves and distributes them equally to everyone. She can also create color stations where leaves of different sizes and a particular color are assigned. Students can move around with their newspaper canvas to create different designs on them.

They could write a line or two of poems dedicated to the beauty of the earth. The teachers can hang them for others to see. Students can use this as an exit ticket. They identify parts of a leaf. Using bubble wrap or cardboard may create a more artistic presentation.

Mapping My Neighborhood: Why Are Units Important? Measure Using Steps and a Trundle Wheel

In idealism, the pursuit of truth, wisdom, and knowledge is a key focus. Utilizing aspects of science, we can help students uncover underlying principles that govern the universe and human existence. Students can be trained to seek the truth through critical thinking and logical reasoning.

The teacher may start with an idea of a famous scientific discovery and discuss how there have been paradigm shifts with the discoveries of Galileo and Isaac Newton. The importance of questioning, reasoning, and understanding is to be discussed.

In this activity, students understand why units are important and learn how to measure using steps and a trundle wheel (or measuring tape). The teacher could start by discussing how they can describe measurements without units—the length of their dress, the width of the book, the height of the building, etc. Then tell them to measure a class corridor or the length of the field using their foot.

Ask them to compare their measurements. Talk about why we need to create a unit system. Ask them to measure the same length using a trundle wheel or a measuring tape. Ask them to compare their measurements.

Now, let students discuss: In which set of measurements were there discrepancies?

Note:

- Teachers can use audiovisual aids like videos to introduce the concept.
- Teachers may use the KWL chart in this activity: what they know, what they want to learn, and what they have learned.
- This activity encourages peer collaboration, which connects real-life examples and makes lessons relatable.

Houses Then and Now: Rural-Urban Differences, Multistoried and Slums

Open Dialogue and Empathy

This is a good opportunity to enhance social connections and encourage empathy among young learners.

The teacher can show pictures of two different buildings in Mumbai (or any other region):

Fig 1

Fig 2

Ask students to discuss what they see. Ask them to note the similarities and the differences between the pictures. Ask students to present their findings.

Show students pictures of slums and newly developed apartments. Ask them to create models of the slums and then create a plan for how to improve living conditions in slums. Students can be helped with a handout/worksheet of key points to discuss, as follows:

What are the features of a slum?	
What problems do slum-dwellers face?	
What could be some improvements that you can suggest?	
What are the materials required to make the model?	

Draw your model plan here:

Ask students to present this as an exhibition and create a video of their explanation. Students reflect on what they have learned and also suggest how they included their own creativity.

While thinking about the problems faced by slum-dwellers, students understand the way of life led by people of all strata of society. They appreciate the advantages that people from the higher strata of society enjoy. The first step of empathy is the appreciation of the differences and advantages of different strata of society.

Journaling for Self-Reflection

A profound example of journaling for self-reflection is Anne Frank's diary. It is a must-have, must-read for all. Get it for your children/students if they don't have it already. It makes a great birthday present for anyone who is mature enough for the story.

Anne processes her thoughts, experiences, and understanding of herself through her diary. Set in the Nazi regime, her brilliance shines under oppressive circumstances. Her relationships, isolations, and revisiting her earlier behaviors are a pristine and pure reflection of her wisdom.

Anne's relentless strive to become a better version of herself is addressed by first showing her anger and then apologizing reflecting on her behavior. She makes peace with her past actions and feelings.

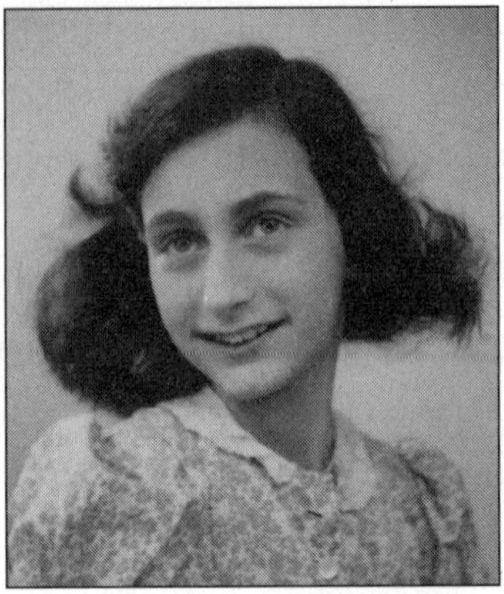

Very interestingly, she writes about how important it is to review one's own behavior, weighing the pros and cons and aiming to better oneself. This is the highlight of the diary's role in Anne's self-reflection and personal development.

On the topic of transport systems in EVS in CBSE, there comes an opportunity for students to journal for reflection.

The students travel with their families during the holidays. They can be asked to journal their travel centered around ways of transport. Create a template for them to document. They need to keep these in mind when they want to journal.

Where are you going?	
How many days are you traveling for?	
In which transport system are you traveling?	
On the day of travel, what are the things that you notice?	

Do you know the occupation of the people who work here?	
Write down how to purchase tickets. What are the restrictions on luggage? Where is this transport system located? How do you board the transport system?	
Collect pictures and stick them in your journal.	

Interdisciplinary Connection

"What happens when I post a letter?"

Students nowadays will have no idea of what it means to 'post' a letter, if we talk about the urban population.

The Postmaster is set in Bengal, where a postmaster who is born in Kolkata is transferred to rural Bengal. There, an orphan girl helps him out with his chores and gives him innocent company. He ultimately has to leave the village when he gets transferred again.

The teacher may use the story to introduce the concept of a post office for a thorough understanding of what a post office is and what a post letter is. Then the teacher can introduce the interdisciplinary teaching plan.

The idea of post letters and offices spans many societal relationships. It starts with the need to communicate with another person. It explores community helpers and binds the disciplines of humanities, arts, science, technology, and value education.

The teacher can start with certain guiding questions:

- What do you understand by the words 'post letter'?
- Have you ever seen a post letter?
- How do you think it reaches someone far away from you?
- What are the people who take them to the receiver called?
- How did people communicate in the past? Research one method from home and come to class.
- How does it differ from the way we send messages today?
- What do you think the mode of sharing information and messages will be in the future?

In doing this activity, the students will be able to think about how technology and processes have evolved. They can also be informed about the floating post office in Kashmir.

Let us explore interdisciplinary connections. When it comes to social studies, we can combine EVS and SST together. Postmen, clerks, and couriers are the community helpers who assist in the process. The post office and courier companies provide us with services. The systems are very efficient, and we can make use of them as needed.

Students can draw a timeline of the evolution of communication:

Pigeon post → telegram → postal mail → email

There are many activities that could help students improve their communication. A trip to the local post office, where they can interview the postal workers to understand the process better, is one such activity. The students can see the different kinds of letters and understand which one is used when—inland letters, postcards, envelopes, greeting cards, etc.

When it comes to interdisciplinary ideas, languages come into the picture. Students may use the English language or the regional language.

They could start learning how to write a letter. Both formal and informal letters can be introduced. The format and etiquette of letter writing are very important for students. It helps them align with how to use language and involves them in the expression of emotions like request, apology, excitement, persuasion, and anger. Writing letters can give them an opportunity to pen their thoughts in an effective way.

In addition to this, they learn how to sign off in a letter and write addresses. Such technical vocabulary of communication is also included.

They would also know what the utility of a stamp is and how the value of the stamp increases the further the letter has to go.

In learning about the history of communication, students improve the art of listening and creative thinking as well.

In languages, students can easily engage with writing a letter to a relative or friend. It could be about their experiences in the interviews that they have conducted at the post office.

Teachers can ask them to read storybooks like *Dear Zoo* or *The Jolly Postman*. Teachers may provide students with a comprehension exercise.

When it comes to art and craft, you may ask students to design personal stationery or draw the template of a letter. They can use decorative paper or ornamental borders to create a letter-writing pad to give to a friend. They could generate a creative representation of the postal system, using drawings, flowcharts, or an idea report on the same.

Activities could include creating your own stamp and explaining what you have included in it. Students could decorate a greeting card as well.

Science and technology can address the evolution of communication, such as how letters were sent manually initially or through trained pigeons. They could appreciate how things have sped up due to technology and how easily we can send a message at the press of a button.

Teachers could also inform the students about the technology of electricity, the internet, and satellites in modern-day messaging. Students may be engaged in activities like making a comparison chart between letters and emails.

The journey of Morse Code could be shown to them via videos. The technology behind the barcode could be introduced to students—what does the barcode scanner do?

Life skills like empathy and gratitude, the importance of networking, reaching out to each other, and the importance of patience in waiting for a reply can also be taught in this activity.

Existentialism

Have you ever seen a movie where a person releases a bird from a cage? Why would he even bother?

What would your students tell you when they see this picture above? Will they be sad? Will they be elated? How would you start explaining what is happening here?

Individual choices and how to own their choices with responsibility is the crux of existentialism. It relies on philosophy and gives a lot of importance to an individual's freedom of choice. The realities of life, exploring their identities, and becoming a responsible individual are what take center stage in this concept.

The Core Principles of Existentialism

Autonomy and empowerment are extremely important for students as this leads to responsibility and a sense of duty. Students may reflect on their interests and choices. A sense of ownership can be inculcated using this concept.

Existentialism also demands authenticity that involves self-discovery and addresses the need to explore one's beliefs, thoughts, and feelings without the fear of judgment. The classroom is a place where each student feels safe and diversity is celebrated. I remember my moral value class in a very strict missionary school, where we could feel extremely safe and heard. As growing teenagers, we shared any concerns with the teacher, who would give us a patient hearing.

Now, when I remember the things I said, I have so much respect for my teacher, as what I said makes no sense to me now. Well, I still judge myself, unlike the classroom steeped in existentialism.

In this context, experiential learning can also be considered—making sense of the experience and assimilating it in their own way. The idea of how the concept makes sense to the student is very interesting.

Responsible behavior and understanding that every action has a consequence are vital to character-building. Discussions of ethical dilemmas and the consequences of their choices can be easily ingrained in the students using the concept of existentialism.

I, for one, wanted to adopt a minimalist way of living. I have tried and failed. Retail therapy has always enticed me, and I'm yet to declare myself a minimalist; I will let you know once I achieve it! That part of existentialism is yet to be established in my life.

Individual Freedom of Choice

In the chapter on 'Family', students are expected to know about their near and dear ones and the relationships they have with the members of the family. The teacher can start with the story of family relationships.

Chapter 1

Family Relationships

I am Angad. I live with the members of my family. They give me love and affection. I share my thoughts and feelings with them. Whenever I am in doubt, I ask my parents, grandparents, uncles or aunts for advice. Sometimes, my siblings or cousins come up with the best advice to make a decision.

Do You Know?
Foster children are not adopted but live with the family for a fixed period.

A 'family' consists of a married couple and their children, both natural (born to that couple) and adopted. Family members share a common residence and surname. Some members of a family may live away from their family home for education, jobs, etc.

The needs of the members are fulfilled by a family. It looks after the children as well as the sick and the old members. All family members love and respect one another.

Do You Know?
Family is the first school where the child learns the **Do's** and the **Don'ts** of the society.

1

The teacher could ask them questions as follows:

- What do the family members do?
- Do the members have pets?
- Who is/are your favorite member(s)?
- Who are you scared of?
- Who do you want to become like? (Maybe they name someone—say, member X)

They are then asked questions that require critical thinking:

- Why do you want to be like member X?
- What are their qualities that make you want to be like them?

They could answer them in a worksheet after a lot of thinking. This helps them delve deep into their choices and think about the humane qualities that they consider important.

In the end, the teacher may create a 'quality cloud' where students write about the qualities that make them want to be like member X.

The teacher can talk about how these qualities help us in life or how they are important for our society.

Self-Discovery

Did you ever have a time during your childhood when you went out to play with the kids in the neighborhood? Every day, and definitely over weekends, there had to be a time when there was unsupervised play. A lot of character-building, understanding right and wrong, self-control, and assessing situations is learned through play.

But the recent changes in our society have seen this 'play' dwindle to a considerable extent. No longer do we see children religiously taking out playtime for themselves. Instead, they have curated classes that would improve their skills—communication, collaboration, critical thinking, and social skills. This is something that happened very organically. I am not complaining—these classes do have robust curricula.

However, the sense of free play can be brought in with a bit of supervision.

In the curriculum of EVS in primary school, there is a topic that deals with games and how we play them. This would give students a lot of liberty and creative space to socialize and work with peers. The environment should provide them with space free of the fear of ridicule or judgment.

For the classroom environment, it helps in building critical thinkers, resilient individuals, and authentic listeners.

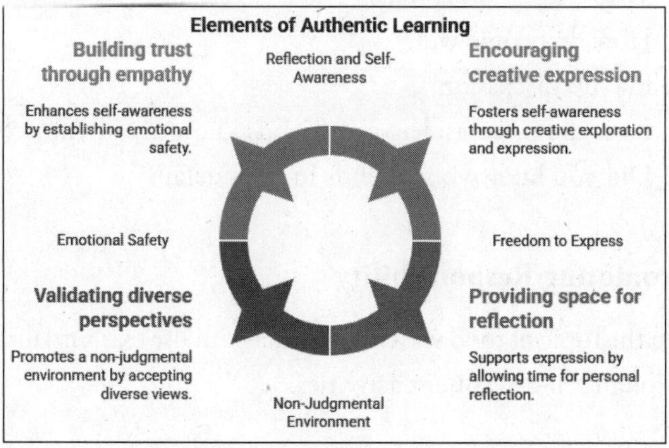

Teaching Idea of Games We Play

Students can create a common game of 'Who am I?' Ask students to write on a chit two truths about themselves and a lie. They have to read them out loud, and their peers will guess the lie.

Name	
Two truths	One lie

The learning is in writing down the rules. Students will volunteer to give rules for the game, and the teacher will facilitate and approve.

- Will it be a group-based activity?
- Who will start?
- How many guesses will be given to each student?
- How many points are scored?
- Who keeps the scores?
- How do people win?

Follow-up discussion:

- How did it feel to let your friends know about yourself?
- Did you know your friends in such detail?

Promoting Responsibility

On the topic of food wastage, teachers can use existentialism through self-assessment activities.

Topic: Food consumption and waste

Self-assessment helps students reflect on themselves. They become aware of their habits and become accountable for their actions. After such activities, students become self-informed and choose responsibly.

A diary of the food we eat: Ask students to maintain a diary for a week, where they log the food they consume. They are given a tracker:

	Monday	Tuesday	Wednesday	Thursday	Friday	Saturday	Sunday
What they eat							
Portion sizes							
Any leftover food?							
Food wasted?							
Reason for food wastage							

Follow-up question: Is there a pattern to your wastage? Which habits will help reduce wastage?

Give them instances of how excess food can be packed with hygiene in mind and given to the needy.

To take it up further, students can establish goal-setting where the objective is to reduce food wastage. The strategy is to teach them the SMART goals: Specific, Measurable, Achievable, Relevant, and Time-bound.

They may think of small portion sizes—measuring portions. How to store leftover food? Dates mentioned to track freshness. Plan what is to be eaten weekly to avoid excess.

For weekly checks to track students' records and progress, the following chart can be used, where the entire class logs the data:

Student	Week	Task	Progress	Notes

Students share this with their peers and understand that they have to maintain it. This builds accountability and a sense of being in control of their choices.

Understanding Agency

In this activity, students are given a scope to understand that choices have consequences. In existentialism, creating a sense of responsibility is highlighted.

We will explore the topic of fun fights and play.

In our world, we all have a Josephine Jones in our lives. The character of *Malory Towers* (a series of children's books by Enid Blyton) who is vicious and manipulative.

- Fun fights and play
- Details on case studies: choices and consequences
- Standing up against bullying
- Scenario: A student witnesses bullying and chooses to intervene by standing up for the victim
- Discussion points
- Positive consequences: Increased respect from peers, improved school environment, emotional support for the victim

Implementation Strategies

- Presenting the case study: Use multimedia tools (videos, articles) or written descriptions to present the case scenario clearly. Ensure that scenarios are relatable and age-appropriate for students.
- Facilitating analysis: Divide students into small groups to discuss the case study. Encourage them to identify choices made by individuals or groups in the scenario and predict potential outcomes.

Building Relationships

How can I stress enough the fact that building relationships opens up so many possibilities in one's life? Networking is the name of the game in today's day and age. The reason is that your connections and network keep you above the usual crowd of people. What you do gets highlighted. People still rely on other people to get information.

So, if you are in need of an opportunity, talk. There might be so much information about other opportunities that you would like to express interest in. You should never shy away from any amount of instruction.

Some inquiry questions can be asked here:

- On which occasions do people eat together?
- On those occasions, which kinds of food are generally eaten?
- Who are the cooks and who are the servers of the food?
- Does your school have a mid-day meal provision?
- Who cooks that?
- Where else have you seen people eating together?
- Is there a celebration associated with eating together?

The teacher may introduce the EVS topic of community eating. The students are informed that sharing food builds bonds and relationships. People gather during social occasions—weddings, parties, feasts, etc.—to celebrate festivals. There is a sense of community here.

The students can be given a short lecture or shown a video on mid-day meals—who initiated it, why it is given to schools, the hygiene maintained, the network of food required for distribution, and the nutritional value of food.

The teacher also emphasizes that different communities eat different types of food. Only on special occasions do we eat special food, which could be family celebrations or rituals.

Teachers can express gratitude for the people who help us cook during these events—our cooks at home, farmers who grow crops, people who deliver groceries, people who serve the food, etc. Without helpers and without networks that transport food, we would never be able to enjoy these occasions.

Teaching Activities

A discussion circle can be formed, where teachers ask questions about recent occasions or festivals. Students are asked to talk about the people gathered, the food they ate, how they enjoyed, etc. Birthday parties are very popular among children. The students can be encouraged to talk about a recent one, and students can also be asked to make a drawing of the occasion, the food served, and who was there.

If the school has a mid-day meal scheme, students can do a mid-day meal observation. They can be asked to journal the school meals for a period of five days. They could talk to the kitchen staff and ask about:

- Where do they get the pulses, grains, rice, etc.?
- How much groceries do they get per month?
- Which items are served?
- What are the plans for serving an item of food each day?
- Who makes the decisions?
- Do you enjoy cooking?

Photo Collage

Students can be asked to collect pictures of food that are specially served in their community during an occasion and eaten by all at a gathering. The teacher may ask them to get a map of India and stick the pictures in the region they belong to—name the occasion, label the region, and write about who cooks it on that day. Examples could be Pongal, shemai, puri sabzi, modak, biryani, etc.

Safety Chart

Ask students to draw up a chart that discusses hygiene in the community kitchen. Students can put up these charts and create awareness about what food hygiene is for others.

Can You Match It?

Foods and festivals associated with the food can be turned into a game. Divide the class into groups. Give them small envelopes that contain pictures of food and festivals associated with that food. Time them and declare the group that gets all the answers correct the fastest as the winner.

In this activity, students identify the festivals and the food related to them. They appreciate cleanliness and hygiene in the preparation of food. They can identify the food and the festivals associated with it. They appreciate the diversity in the community.

Students learn how to respect the work of all types. Ideas of inclusivity and empathy for the hard work that farmers do, as well as appreciation for all the work people do to bring food to our table, are addressed.

Authentic Problem-Solving

Authentic problem-solving can be accomplished in various ways. We can look at real-world learning, experiential learning, and inquiry-based learning.

Authentic problem-solving has real-life problems at its core. Children can be involved in actively working to solve these problems. The skills that can be improved are the power of observation, collaboration, thinking while making decisions, and discussions to come to a consensus.

Using it in EVS makes the learning relevant and impactful. Student agency—choice, voice, and ownership—increases as they engage in something that will create meaningful learning in their lives. It encourages a sense of empathy. Students also connect other subjects and concepts together.

Theme 1: Tap water leakage in the community. It brings together ideas of wastage and conservation of natural resources. Students are asked to take turns observing a tap that leaks water and maybe collect the amount of water leaked in an hour. They can multiply that by 24 to determine the loss per day.

They may write a letter to the community head to fix the tap and draw attention to how the water lost per day is precious and should be taken care of.

Theme 2: Plastic-plastic everywhere. Students could observe or audit the number of plastic lunchboxes or plastic bottles in school. Cling-film is also another product that could be looked into. They can campaign by creating a poster in school about reducing the use of plastic. Teachers can talk about how microplastics are found in human stomachs.

Theme 3: Where have the trees gone?

Interview with parents/guardians/grandparents.

Teachers can tell students to ask their elders about the place they live in.

Was it always the same?

What has changed in recent years?

Do they see less trees?

Why were the trees cut?

Can they not plant tree saplings in their locality?

Students are asked to explain to their elders and urge them to plant saplings in the nearby areas. They can go with them on a Sunday and plant them with permission from the local administrator.

Tell students to read up on how to make a kitchen garden. They should ask their mothers/grandmothers/aunts to make a kitchen garden for fresh herbs.

Theme 4: Is that street dog hurt? What are the steps that need to be taken when you see an injured animal in your neighborhood? Students turn empathetic toward all living things around them. Helpless, injured animals would also be considered.

Teachers may tell them to look up the names of NGOs that help animals in such conditions in case of emergencies. The school can take them to animal shelters where people from the NGO can talk to them about their processes of helping rescued animals.

In order to execute these thematic activities, teachers can use tools like peer discussion strategies, observation sheets, interviews, roleplays, resource persons in the locality, charts, journals, and photos.

Chapter 5

AI and Coding for Young Learners – An NEP-Friendly Introduction

Why AI and Coding in Primary School?

The National Education Policy (NEP) 2020 emphasizes the need to prepare children for the future by building 21st-century skills such as problem-solving, logical reasoning, creativity, and digital literacy. While concepts like Artificial Intelligence (AI) and Coding may sound advanced, they can be introduced at the primary level in age-appropriate and playful ways.

For Classes 3–5, the aim is not to make children expert programmers but to:

- Develop computational thinking (breaking problems into steps).
- Encourage pattern recognition and logical reasoning.
- Introduce them to the idea of "machines that can think" through simple, everyday examples.
- Build curiosity and comfort with technology.

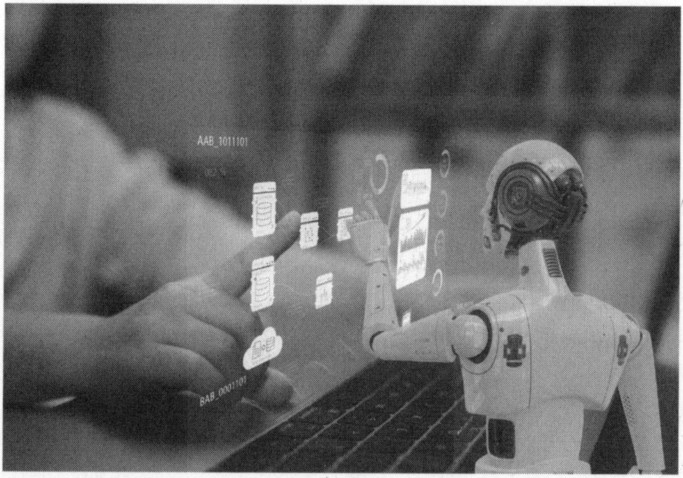

What is AI?

AI means teaching machines to 'think' or 'learn' like humans. For children, AI can be explained through examples they already use daily:

- Voice assistants (Alexa, Siri, Google Assistant).
- YouTube recommendations.
- Spell check and auto-correct.
- Face unlock on mobile phones.

Imagine you have a puppy. At first, your puppy doesn't know how to sit, fetch, or roll over. But if you keep repeating the command and reward it when it does the right thing, the puppy slowly learns.

AI works the same way. A computer doesn't 'know' anything at first. But when we give it many examples and show it what is right or wrong, it learns, just like a pet.

- **Teaching a Dog to Sit**
    - You say 'Sit' but dog may or may not sit.
    - If the dog sits, you give a treat and the dog learns that 'sit' means reward.
    - After practice, the dog can sit when asked.
- **Training AI to Recognize a Cat**
    - You show the computer many pictures of cats and sometimes it guesses right, sometimes wrong.
    - If it's right, we say 'Yes, that's correct.'
    - If it's wrong, we correct it.
    - After many examples, the AI learns to recognize a cat.

The puppy and the AI both learn by practice, feedback and correction.

What is Coding?

Coding is giving step-by-step instructions to a computer so it can perform a task. It is like writing a recipe for a computer to follow.

For Classes 3 – 5, coding is best introduced through:

- Block-based coding platforms (Scratch, Blockly, Code.org).

- Game-based activities (Minecraft Education Edition, Tynker).
- Unplugged coding – coding without computers, using arrows, cards, or floor grids.

Pedagogical Approaches (Aligned to NEP 2020)

Activity-Based Learning:

- Use puzzles, mazes, and pattern games to introduce sequencing.
- Example: Ask students to guide a 'robot friend' (teacher or toy) across the classroom using directional commands (forward, left, right).
- Play-Based Coding
- Use coding toys (Bee-Bots, Lego WeDo, or affordable Indian alternatives).
- Online block-based coding can start in Grade 4 – 5 with simple animations (Scratch Jr).

Integrating AI into Everyday Lessons:

NEP 2020 encourages blended, real-world learning, where students see how classroom knowledge connects to life around them. AI, though often thought of as 'futuristic,' is already present in tools children use every day. Teachers can integrate AI examples into science without needing special equipment. Just curiosity, conversation and simple demonstrations.

Activity: Weather Prediction with AI

Classroom Connection: In Environmental Science, students often study weather, seasons and climate. Teachers can connect this to AI by showing how apps on smartphones predict the weather.

- **Teacher Demo:** Open a weather app and show the class today's temperature and tomorrow's forecast. Ask: *'How does the app know what the weather will be tomorrow?'*
- **Discussion:** Explain that AI learns from thousands of data points (like past temperature, rainfall and wind speed) and uses patterns to make predictions.
- **Activity Idea:** Have students keep a weather journal for a week, write the forecast vs. the actual weather, and compare. This helps them see how prediction works: sometimes accurate, sometimes not (just like learning).
- **Skill Link:** Observation, data recording, pattern recognition and understanding uncertainty.

NEP Connection: Builds inquiry, connects science to technology and links local context (weather outside the classroom) with global tools.

Teacher Tip Box

- Always remind students: AI is a tool, not a teacher.
- Encourage children to question results (Is the forecast always right? Did the chatbot solve the problem correctly? Did the translation make sense?).
- Use AI to spark curiosity, not replace classroom learning.

Sample Classroom Activities: AI and Coding

These activities are designed to make AI and coding playful, experiential and age-appropriate. They can be done in any school environment, even with limited resources. Each activity includes objectives, materials, steps and reflection.

1. Unplugged Coding Game (Class 3)

Materials:

- A floor grid (5 × 5 squares made with chalk, tape, or chart paper).
- Paper arrows (↑, →, ←, ↓).
- A small toy (animal, car or block).
- A picture card representing 'food' or 'goal.'

Objective:

- To introduce coding as giving step-by-step instructions.
- To build sequencing, logical reasoning and teamwork.

Steps:

1. Place the toy on one square of the grid and the 'goal' on another square.
2. Ask students to 'code' the toy's movement using arrow cards (e.g., ↑↑→→↓).
3. One student lays down the code, another student 'executes' it by moving the toy.
4. If the toy misses the goal, debug together by correcting the code.

Discussion Prompts:

- 'What happened when the toy didn't reach the food?'
- 'How is this like telling a computer what to do?'
- 'Why is order important in coding?'

Variations:

- Add obstacles on the grid (rocks, rivers) for more challenge.
- Make it a team race: two groups code the fastest path.

2. Scratch Jr Animation (Class 4)

Materials:

- Tablets/laptops with Scratch Jr app installed.
- Basic tutorial sheet (move, loop, start).

Task:

Students create a short animation where the Sun rises and a flower blooms.

Steps:

1. Demonstrate how to add characters (Sun, flower).
2. Show basic blocks: move, grow, wait, repeat.
3. Guide students to:
    - Make the Sun move upward.
    - Make the flower 'grow' and 'open.'
    - Add background (sky changing color).
4. Let students add their own creative touches (a bee flying, a cloud passing).

Learning:

- Understanding sequencing, loops, cause-effect.
- Creativity in storytelling with code.

Reflection Prompts:

- 'What happens if we change the order of blocks?'
- 'How is coding like writing a story?'

Variations:

- Create a short story (day → night).
- Add sound effects or dialogue.

3. AI in Daily Life

Materials:

- A smartphone with Google Lens or a voice assistant (Google Assistant, Alexa, Siri).
- A few natural/environmental objects (leaf, flower, seed, bottle of water, piece of paper).
- Chart paper and markers.

Activity:

1. Use the voice assistant to ask:
    - *'What is today's air quality in our city?'*
    - *'When is the sunrise/sunset today?'*
    - *'What is the weather tomorrow?'*
2. Use Google Lens to scan a leaf or flower and see how AI identifies the plant.

3. **Ask:** *'How does the AI know the name of this plant or today's weather?'*
   - **Explain simply:** 'The AI has learned from thousands of weather records or plant photos, just like students learn from many practice exercises. It's like training a pet, but here the computer is being trained.'

Discussion Prompts:

- *'Does the AI always get it right? What if it confuses two plants?'*
- *'How is this similar to how we sometimes make mistakes in class?'*
- *'How could AI help us care for the environment (e.g., predicting rainfall, identifying endangered plants)?'*
- *'Can AI replace human care for nature, or do we still need people to protect it?'*

Extension:

- Compare AI's plant identification with what students know: are they the same?
- Roleplay: Students act as 'human AI'. One student listens to a weather question, another checks a chart or a poster and a third gives the answer. Discuss how data is needed before an answer can be given.
- Mini project: *'If I had an AI friend for the Earth, what could it do?'* (ideas: detect waste, water plants, save electricity, warn about pollution). Students can draw or write their ideas.

Teacher Reflection Section

- Which activity worked best for my class?
- How did students respond to AI/coding concepts?
- Did students show curiosity beyond the activity?
- How can I link these ideas to my regular syllabus?

Chapter 6

Checking for Understanding

Teaching Environmental Science is not only about delivering information but about ensuring that every child makes sense of what they have learned. Checking for Understanding (CFU) is the teacher's way of pausing, observing, and confirming: *Do my students really understand this concept?* This step is especially important in Classes 3 – 5, where children are developing critical thinking, curiosity and connections with their immediate environment. CFU enables a more responsive classroom, fostering a culture of continuous feedback and improvement.

> Barak Rosenshine, professor of educational psychology, asserts that effective teaching involves asking questions and checking students' responses to help them practice new information and connect it with their prior knowledge. Rosenshine's research suggests that teachers should ask questions during instruction to facilitate the practice of new material. The most effective teachers engage all students by having them share answers with peers, summarise points, write responses or express agreement with others. CFU is key to ensure that the knowledge being transferred to long-term memory is correct.

Why It Matters

- Many children can repeat facts (e.g., 'plants give us oxygen'), but real understanding means they can *apply* it (e.g., 'if many trees are cut, air quality becomes poor').
- Misconceptions in EVS are common (e.g., 'the Sun rises in the east because it moves around the Earth'). Catching these early prevents confusion later.
- The NEP 2020 emphasizes competency-based learning and joyful education, where understanding is deeper than rote memorization.

How does one implement it?

- **Use a range of questioning:** A straightforward and effective method for assessing student knowledge is thorough questioning. Teachers can employ various questioning strategies to check understanding. These include cold calling students and asking follow up questions to probe their knowledge: 'Why do you think that is?'. Elaborative interrogation questions such as 'Why is this true?' are also powerful to check the depth of students' understanding and help them connect their knowledge to existing schema.
- **Provide Choice Statements:** Present students with a few choice statements of questions and ask them to select a response. For example, 'true or false', 'agree or disagree' and share it via a mini-whiteboard, or hand

signal (thumbs up or down). This technique is especially useful in gauging students' prior knowledge or potential misconceptions before beginning new instruction. It also encourages learners to elaborate on the material and make connections to other learning in their long-term memory.

- **Correcting Exercises:** A highly efficient and effective method for checking students' understanding is through identifying and rectifying errors and misconceptions. Present an incorrect example and ask students to correct it individually or in pairs. Circulate the room and check for understanding.
- **Create Visual Representations:** Graphic organisers and concept maps can be useful for checking the depth of students' understanding. Encourage students to create a visual or symbolic representation (for example a graphic organizer, simple table, or concept map) of information and abstract concepts and then have them prepare to discuss their graphics with a partner. Picturing techniques are useful to see if students understand how various concepts or elements of a process are related. It is important to model and rehearse this process so that students know how to create effective visual maps independently.

Questioning Techniques

Avoid only asking 'What is…?' Instead, try:

- *'What would happen if it didn't rain for one year?'*
- *'Why do we need to plant trees near our school?'*

Encourage multiple answers, not just the 'correct' one.

Practical Strategies to Check Understanding

1. Think–Pair–Share

- **Process:** After a short lesson (e.g., on water conservation), ask students to think of one example from home, pair with a classmate to discuss, then share with the class.
- **Why it works:** Even shy children get to process their ideas before speaking.

2. Concept Mapping

- **Activity:** Ask students to draw a simple map linking 'Sun → Plants → Animals → Humans.'
- **Purpose:** Reveals how children connect ideas about food chains or interdependence.
- **Tip:** Encourage arrows, drawings and words. Not just text.

3. Exit Tickets

- **Method:** At the end of class, ask one quick question:
  - 'Write one way you saved water at home this week.'
  - 'Draw something in nature that breathes air.'

- Students submit answers on slips of paper before leaving.
- **Advantage:** Gives the teacher instant feedback on which children grasped the day's concept.

4. Role Play and Simulation

- **Example:** In a lesson on pollution, assign roles: 'You are a tree,' 'You are smoke from a car,' 'You are clean air.' Ask them to act out interactions.
- **Check:** Observe whether children can explain what happens when smoke surrounds the tree.

5. Peer Teaching

- **Activity:** After teaching 'Sources of Water,' ask one group to explain it to another group using a drawing or short skit.
- **Benefit:** Teaching forces children to clarify their own understanding.

6. Everyday Connections

- **Ask:** *'How is the fan in your home like the wind?'* or '*What happens in your kitchen when water boils?'*
- This helps assess whether children can link classroom learning to real life.

Activity 1: Look at both the images. Ask: 'Which is a living thing?' 'Which is a non-living thing?'. Easy, right? But also ask the students to explain why. Give them one or two minutes to think quietly, then discuss in pairs and finally share the answers with the class. The expected responses usually are: the tree is living because it grows, needs water and can make food or the bicycle is non-living because it does breathe, eat or grow. Some children may say the bicycle is 'living' because it moves (It only moves when humans push or ride it). Some may say the tree is 'non-living' because it doesn't walk (living things don't need to move like humans to be alive).

Ask students to add one more example of a living thing and one non-living thing from their own surroundings. Create a 'Living vs. Non-Living' wall-chart where children stick drawings of magazine cut-outs in the correct column.

It's a simple enough lesson but it becomes a full mini-knowledge check that is useful for both assessment and deeper engagement.

Activity 2:

Bring or draw 3 bins on the board (Green – Wet Waste, Blue – Dry Waste and Red – Hazardous). Show some objects or if you wish to have more fun draw them on the blackboard: banana peels, plastic bottles, broken glass, newspaper. Now ask your students 'Which bin will each item go into? Why?'

Some expected responses will be:

Banana peel → Green (because it rots/composts).

Plastic bottle → Blue (dry recyclable).

Broken glass → Red (hazardous).

Newspaper → Blue (recyclable).

Check possible misconceptions. Students may put glass into the blue bin because it's 'recyclable". Clarify that glass is recyclable but dangerous, so it goes int hazardous bins first. Some may confuse wet vs. dry waste. Reinforce that wet waste is for waste that decomposes quickly and dry waste is for waste that does not. Ask them to bring on object from their school bag such as a wrapper, pencil shaving, paper scrap and sort it into the right 'imaginary bin'.

Activity 3:

Draw a simple diagram of clouds, Sun, water body and rain on the board. Now ask your students: Imagine the Sun does not shine for 10 days. Which part of the water cycle will stop first? Why? Let them explain in pairs, then share.

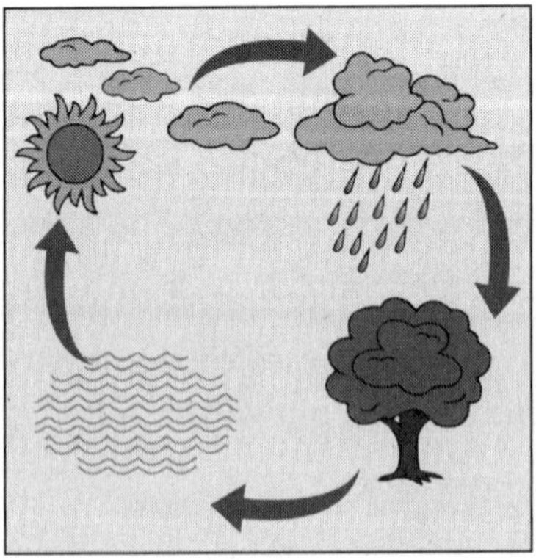

The expected responses will be that evaporation will stop because water needs heat from the Sun or if evaporations stops, clouds will not form, so no rain later. However, some possible misconceptions may arise such as 'Rain will stop immediately'. Clarify that stored water in clouds may still fall as rain for some days. Some may even think that the Sun 'creates' water, so it is better to clarify that it only provides energy to move water around.

This way, checking for understanding is not an 'extra step' but the heart of good teaching. When teachers take time to see what children have truly learned, lessons become meaningful and students grow as curious, confident learners who can care for the environment and connect science to their everyday lives.

Chapter 7

Glossary of Pedagogical Terms

1. **Inquiry-Based Learning:** A method where students explore questions and problems about the environment rather than being given facts directly.
2. **Experiential Learning:** Hands-on, real-world experiences (e.g., planting seeds, observing weather) to build understanding.
3. **Constructivism:** The idea that children build knowledge by connecting new concepts to their own experiences.
4. **Place-Based Learning:** Using the local environment (school garden, park, community) as a primary resource for science learning.
5. **Interdisciplinary Approach:** Linking Environmental Science with math, art, language, or social studies to give holistic learning.
6. **Project-Based Learning (PBL):** Long-term projects such as "Waste Management in My School" to encourage problem-solving and collaboration.
7. **Activity-Based Pedagogy:** Using experiments, role plays, games, and activities to make environmental concepts concrete.

8. **Observation Skills:** Training children to notice patterns in plants, animals, weather, and surroundings systematically.
9. **Concept Mapping:** Visual diagrams that help students connect ideas like "water → plants → food → humans."
10. **Scientific Temper:** Cultivating curiosity, evidence-seeking, and rational thinking in young learners.
11. **Collaborative Learning:** Small group tasks where students learn from each other (e.g., preparing a class chart on seasons).
12. **Experiments with Everyday Materials:** Hands-on investigations using common objects (bottles, soil, leaves, sunlight).
13. **Problem-Posing Education:** Presenting real-world environmental problems (pollution, waste, energy use) for children to discuss solutions.
14. **Scaffolding:** Teacher support that helps students move from guided observation to independent investigation.
15. **Reflective Practice:** Encouraging children to think about what they learned and how it applies to daily life.
16. **Citizen Science:** Simple classroom projects that contribute to larger community knowledge (e.g., recording bird sightings).
17. **Value-Based Education:** Linking environmental studies with values like empathy, conservation, and responsibility.

18. **Systems Thinking:** Understanding how different parts of nature (soil, water, air, plants, animals, humans) are interconnected.
19. **Sustainability Education:** Teaching children the importance of conserving resources and caring for the planet.
20. **Experiential Assessment:** Evaluating through projects, portfolios, or presentations rather than only written tests.
21. **Hands-on Learning:** Direct engagement with materials (soil, leaves, seeds, water) to explore concepts actively.
22. **Inquiry Cycle:** A structured process of Ask → Investigate → Record → Reflect → Share for young learners.
23. **Experiential Storytelling:** Using narratives or folk tales to explain environmental phenomena (e.g., water cycle as a journey).
24. **Sensory Learning:** Engaging sight, sound, touch, and smell in environmental exploration (e.g., "sound walk" in the schoolyard).
25. **Formative Assessment:** Continuous evaluation through quizzes, drawings, observations, and peer discussions.
26. **Experiments-in-Pairs:** Small group or buddy-based activities to promote peer support and collaboration.
27. **STEAM Integration:** Connecting science with technology, engineering, art, and math (e.g., building a rainwater model).

28. **Experiential Play:** Using games and playful exploration to introduce environmental concepts.
29. **Learning by Doing:** A pedagogy rooted in activity (planting, recycling, observing) rather than rote memorization.
30. **Environmental Ethics:** Teaching respect, care, and responsibility towards nature through everyday classroom practices.

Chapter 8

Conclusion

As we close this book, one truth becomes clear: teaching is both a science and an art. From behaviorism to cognitivism, from idealism to AI-driven innovation, every perspective offers teachers a lens through which to shape learning. No single method stands alone; rather, effective teaching in Environmental Science and beyond comes from weaving these approaches together with wisdom and sensitivity to children's needs.

The NEP 2020 vision reminds us that education in India must be:

- Competency-based rather than rote-driven,
- Joyful and experiential rather than exam-centered,
- Connected to life and the environment rather than confined to textbooks.

The chapters in this book are stepping stones toward this vision. Behaviorism helps us understand how reinforcement shapes habits; cognitivism shows us how children process and organize knowledge; idealism keeps alive the values, ethics, and larger purposes of education. Practical tools like

Checking for Understanding remind us that children learn best when teachers actively listen to their thinking. And forward-looking ideas like AI and coding open the classroom to the future: preparing even young learners to live, work and solve problems in a world shaped by technology.

At its heart, this book is about empowering teachers:

- To build classrooms where curiosity is celebrated,
- To nurture critical thinking while respecting local culture and context,
- To guide every child toward becoming not just a knowledgeable student, but also a responsible citizen who can care for the environment and society.

In the end, teaching for Classes 3 – 5 is not simply about explaining the water cycle, waste segregation or living and non-living things. It is about building the habit of asking questions, connecting ideas, and caring for the Earth. When teachers blend sound pedagogy with compassion, creativity and the courage to innovate, they not only implement NEP 2020 but also prepare children for lives of meaning, responsibility and lifelong learning.

This book is only a beginning. The journey of an educator continues in every lesson, every 'question a child asks and every smile of recognition when a concept 'clicks. May it inspire teachers to keep reflecting, keep experimenting and keep reimagining classrooms, for the children of today and the India of tomorrow.

Notes

1. https://www.linkedin.com/advice/3/how-do-you-use-critical-pedagogy-your-teaching
2. https://www.indeed.com/career-advice/career-development/ strategies-for-teachers
3. https://digitalcommons.unl.edu/cgi/viewcontent.cgi?article=1155&context=teachlearnfacpub
4. https://schools.magoosh.com/schools-blog/top-10-teaching-strategies
5. https://en.wikipedia.org/wiki/Critical_pedagogy
6. https://www.prodigygame.com/main-cn/blog/teaching-strategies/
7. https://study.com/academy/lesson/critical-pedagogy-in-the-classroom.html
8. https://thirdspacelearning.com/blog/teaching-strategies/
9. https://www.frontiersin.org/journals/plant-science/articles/10.3389/fpls.2017.02069/full
10. https://www.audubon.org/news/what-difference-between-native-non-native-and-invasive-plants
11. https://emswcd.org/native-plants/native-plant-benefits/
12. https://www.saintleo.edu/about/stories/blog/socratic-method-teaching-what-it-its-benefits-and-examples
13. https://www.ascd.org/el/articles/the-socratic-approach-to-character-education

14. https://www.dcr.virginia.gov/natural-heritage/benefits
15. https://lessonbud.com/blog/the-socratic-method-engaging-students-in-critical-thinking-and-dialogue/
16. https://blog.bjupress.com/blog/2021/06/08/socratic-method-of-teaching/
17. https://www.britannica.com/topic/Socratic-method
18. https://www.quadratacademy.com/single-post/the-socratic-method-what-it-is-and-how-to-use-it-in-the-classroom
19. https://study.com/learn/lesson/socractic-dialogue-examples.html
20. https://www.edutopia.org/article/using-socratic-method-your-classroom/
21. https://blog.landscapeprofessionals.org/sustainability-native-versus-non-native-plants/
22. https://www.latrobe.edu.au/news/announcements/2021/gardening-tips-5-reasons-to-grow-indigenous-plants
23. https://www.rhs.org.uk/prevention-protection/invasive-non-native-plants
24. https://www.lawnstarter.com/blog/landscaping/benefits-native-plants/
25. https://www.wildflower.org/learn/guide-native-plant-gardening
26. https://lawnlove.com/blog/reasons-to-grow-native-plants/

27. https://en.wikipedia.org/wiki/Socratic_questioning
28. https://www.joinprisma.com/blog/what-is-the-socratic-method-for-kids
29. https://www.fs.usda.gov/wildflowers/Native_Plant_Materials/Native_Gardening/instructions.shtml
30. https://pmc.ncbi.nlm.nih.gov/articles/PMC5723411/
31. https://pmc.ncbi.nlm.nih.gov/articles/PMC7882654/
32. https://www.dcr.virginia.gov/natural-heritage/native-vs-aliens
33. https://extension.psu.edu/why-use-native-plants
34. https://www.hcn.org/issues/the-complex-case-of-growing-native-plants/
35. https://defenders.org/blog/2024/04/benefits-of-planting-native-plants
36. https://pmc.ncbi.nlm.nih.gov/articles/PMC9618556/
37. https://www.newindianexpress.com/magazine/2024/Aug/17/kolkatas-food-atm-initiative-fights-hunger-reduces-food-waste#:~:text=A%20call%20comes%20in%20to%20Kolkata%20We,surplus%20food%20that%20needs%20to%20be%20collected.&text=The%20purpose%20of%20this%20timely%20intervention%2C%20a,food%20waste%20in%20the%20City%20of%20Joy. https://www.linkedin.com/pulse/cognitive-teaching-strategies-social-science-dr-dinesh-chauhan
38. https://pmc.ncbi.nlm.nih.gov/articles/PMC6946583/
39. https://www.valamis.com/hub/cognitive-learning

40. https://study.com/academy/lesson/cognitive-learning-theory-examples.html
41. https://www.open.edu/openlearncreate/mod/page/view.php?id=147079
42. https://study.com/cimages/multimages/16/cognitivepsychology.svg2361993676230721779.png?sa=X&ved=2ahUKEwi_6_Wquo6LAxWEElkFHQrfHhQQ_B16BAgCEAI
43. https://www.structural-learning.com/post/cognitivism-learning-theories
44. https://cognassist.com/insights/cognitive-strategies/
45. https://thirst.io/blog/what-is-cognitive-learning-theory/
46. https://www.educate-me.co/blog/knowledge-retention-strategies
47. https://cognassist.com/insights/cognitive-strategies/
48. https://in.indeed.com/career-advice/career-development/cognitive-learning https://pmc.ncbi.nlm.nih.gov/articles/PMC6946583/
49. https://www.valamis.com/hub/cognitive-learning
50. https://www.researchgate.net/publication/336950380_Applying_Cognitive_Learning_Strategies_to_Enhance_Learning_and_Retention_in_Clinical_Teaching_Settings
51. https://whatfix.com/blog/learning-retention/
52. https://www.phoenix.edu/blog/what-is-cognitive-learning-theory.html

53. https://www.linkedin.com/pulse/cognitive-teaching-strategies-social-science-dr-dinesh-chauhan/
54. https://educationaltechnology.net/cognitivism-learning-theory-strategies-and-examples/
55. https://www.valamis.com/hub/cognitive-learning
56. https://www.open.edu/openlearncreate/mod/page/view.php?id=147079
57. https://www.prodigygame.com/main-en/blog/inquiry-based-learning-definition-benefits-strategies/
58. https://www.buffalo.edu/catt/teach/develop/theory/constructivism.html#title_1308821097
59. https://www.simplypsychology.org/constructivism.html#Critical-Evaluation
60. https://files.eric.ed.gov/fulltext/EJ1241559.pdf
61. http://davcae.net.in/File/cls-4%2056.pdf
62. https://researchoutreach.org/articles/pushing-boundaries-peter-mclaren-importance-critical-pedagogy-inside-outside-classroom/
63. https://www.natgeokids.com/uk/kids-club/cool-kids/general-kids-club/greta-thunberg-facts/
64. https://tlhub.stanford.edu/docs/conducting-role-plays/
65. https://serc.carleton.edu/introgeo/interactive/roleplay.html
66. https://www.trainingforchange.org/training_tools/how-to-lead-roleplays/
67. https://blogs.shu.ac.uk/shutel/2014/07/04/role-play-an-approach-to-teaching-and-learning/

68. https://serc.carleton.edu/introgeo/roleplaying/howto.html
69. https://www.edutopia.org/blog/role-play-sel-teaching-tool-kristin-stuart-valdes
70. https://www.niu.edu/citl/resources/guides/instructional-guide/role-playing.shtml
71. https://www.zinnedproject.org/news/how-to-teach-role-plays/
72. https://pmc.ncbi.nlm.nih.gov/articles/PMC9736355/
73. https://pmc.ncbi.nlm.nih.gov/articles/PMC9942952/
74. https://pmc.ncbi.nlm.nih.gov/articles/PMC1847843/
75. https://www.psa.ac.uk/sites/default/files/conference/papers/2015/Being%20an%20Environmental%20Idealist%20bullet%20points.pdf
76. https://www.mdpi.com/2071-1050/16/7/2707
77. https://www.mdpi.com/2227-7102/9/1/37
78. https://www.mdpi.com/2409-9287/6/4/91
79. https://www.sundayobserver.lk/2024/07/21/news-features/28285/the-benefits-of-aesthetic-qualities-and-humanities-education/
80. https://www.cuny.edu/wp-content/uploads/sites/4/page-assets/about/administration/offices/undergraduate-studies/pathways/about/archive/resources/lo/Math_Humanities_Learning_Outcomes_Examples.pdf
81. https://www.ie.edu/uncover-ie/extracurricular-activities-in-the-humanities-building-skills-for-a-better-future/
82. https://makeandtakes.com/leaf-printing-card-making

83. https://www.polygence.org/blog/arts-and-humanities-passion-project-ideas-for-students
84. https://www.clothpaperscissors.com/blog/nature-print-greeting-card-tutorial/
85. https://www.postcrossing.com/blog/2024/11/14/leaf-printing-tutorial
86. https://education.theiet.org/primary/teaching-resources/make-a-leaf-print
87. https://www.straighterline.com/blog/what-are-humanities-classes
88. https://www.greatassignmenthelp.com/blog/humanities-research-topics/
89. https://www.instructables.com/Let-us-green-you-up-Handmade-paper-planter-cards/
90. https://www.youtube.com/watch?v=9-jKA82iZKg
91. https://www.freepik.com/vectors/unique-earth-day-card-ideas
92. https://www.earthday.org/earth-day-cards/
93. https://human.libretexts.org/Courses/Sauk_Valley_Community_College/HUM_210:_Humanities_I-Intro_to_the_Arts/01:_Introduction_to_the_Arts/1.08:_An_Introduction_to_the_Arts_and_Humanities
94. https://augstudy.com/what-is-arts-and-humanities/
95. https://www.assignmenthelppro.com/blog/humanities-research-topics/
96. https://plato.stanford.edu/entries/art-definition/

97. https://www.printique.com/blog/celebrate-earth-day-in-print-5-ideas/
98. https://cbseacademic.nic.in/web_material/Manuals/Teachers_handbook-Science.pdf
99. https://www.care.com/c/12-must-follow-principles-for-teaching-scienc/
100. https://www.teachhub.com/teaching-strategies/2014/09/teaching-strategies-to-promote-critical-thinking/
101. https://schoolsequella.det.nsw.edu.au/file/ce0d6d8b-7d38-487e-b42b-b264e90aec18/1/teaching-measurement-S2-S3.pdf
102. https://cms-im.s3.amazonaws.com/lrb98sn5sdzd9ntt1ubap8x2bgi1?response-content-disposition=inline%3B+filename%3D%22Grade7-9-12-Lesson-teacher-guide.pdf%22%3B+filename%2A%3DUTF-8%27%27Grade7-9-12-Lesson-teacher-guide.pdf&response-content-type=application%2Fpdf&X-Amz-Algorithm=AWS4-HMAC-SHA256&X-Amz-Credential=AKIAXQCCIHWF3XOEFOW4%2F20241029%2Fus-east-1%2Fs3%2Faws4_request&X-Amz-Date=20241029T005106Z&X-Amz-Expires=604800&X-Amz-SignedHeaders=host&X-Amz-Signature=a1959cd5c785acc1a459aefed4616f0a40e24a993c4fbfa5fd917b5c8dcd9436

103. https://math.libretexts.org/Bookshelves/PreAlgebra/Pre-Algebra_I_(Illustrative_Mathematics_-_Grade_7)/09:_Untitled_Chapter_9/9.03:_New_Page/9.3.3:_Using_a_Trundle_Wheel_to_Measure_Distances
104. https://www.pw.live/exams/wp-content/uploads/2024/03/CBSE-Class-6-Science-Notes-Chapter-10-1.pdf
105. https://im.kendallhunt.com/MS/teachers/2/9/11/index.html
106. https://im.kendallhunt.com/MS/teachers/2/9/12/index.html
107. https://www.youtube.com/watch?v=Tsee60XpD60
108. https://academic.oup.com/book/44534/chapter/376956419
109. https://sulur.kvs.ac.in
110. https://www.vedantu.com/physics/our-universe
111. https://www.youtube.com/watch?v=eQDQ4CxUEc0
112. https://www.youtube.com/watch?v=e7259fqXnQw
113. https://pmc.ncbi.nlm.nih.gov/articles/PMC4710388/
114. https://www.extramarks.com/studymaterials/cbse/cbse-class-11-physics-revision-notes-chapter-2/
115. https://www.youtube.com/watch?v=VMu-cDn93Tg
116. https://education.lego.com/en-us/lessons/spm/trundle-wheel/

117. https://byjus.com/cbse-notes/cbse-class-6-science-notes-chapter-10-motion-and-measurement-of-distances/
118. https://cdnbbsr.s3waas.gov.in/s3kv029a7b1fa8050badd7a541cf5ca96b/uploads/2024/09/2024091936.pdf
119. https://www.youtube.com/watch?v=b8rrE4u_-TA
120. https://ncert.nic.in/pdf/NCF_for_Foundational_Stage_20_October_2022.pdf
121. https://pmc.ncbi.nlm.nih.gov/articles/PMC8223544/
122. https://cbseit.in/cbse/2022/ET/assets1/pdf/NCF_SE.pdf
123. https://cbseacademic.nic.in/cbe/documents/Learning_Standards_Science.pdf
124. https://www.cbse.gov.in/cbsenew/documents/Handbook_for_students.pdf
125. https://cas.sdss.org/dr7/en/proj/teachers/basic/universe/lesson.asp
126. https://mycbseguide.com/blog/how-to-create-a-lesson-plan-for-cbse-class-10-science/
127. https://byjus.com/cbse/cbse-class-6-to-8-science-lab-manuals/
128. https://www.jagranjosh.com/articles/cbse-class-10-science-teacher-lesson-plan-pdf-1715325540-1
129. https://cbseacademic.nic.in/cbe/documents/Lesson-Plan-Science-Final.pdf

130. https://www.cbse.gov.in/publications/science_activity_class_viii.pdf
131. https://www.middleweb.com/33888/helping-students-develop-logical-reasoning/
132. https://www.edweek.org/teaching-learning/opinion-eight-instructional-strategies-for-promoting-critical-thinking/2021/03
133. https://www.waldenu.edu/online-bachelors-programs/bs-in-elementary-education/resource/seven-ways-to-teach-critical-thinking-in-elementary-education
134. https://swgfl.org.uk/magazine/logical-reasoning-across-the-primary-curriculum/
135. https://study.com/academy/lesson/teaching-critical-thinking-skills.html
136. https://mathgeekmama.com/how-to-teach-logical-reasoning/
137. https://files.eric.ed.gov/fulltext/ED575667.pdf
138. https://www.thegaudium.com/the-importance-of-teaching-children-to-read-maps/
139. https://www.youtube.com/watch?v=q8Xsut5BgSU
140. https://www.youtube.com/watch?v=UZBLTeDbrqY
141. https://byjus.com/cbse-notes/class-11-physics-notes-units-measurements/
142. https://www.vedantu.com/revision-notes/cbse-class-11-physics-notes-chapter-1-units-and-measurement

143. https://www.youtube.com/watch?v=O1hPisdsDtI
144. https://www.youtube.com/watch?v=Fj16hf-iF0U
145. https://www.geogebra.org/m/vpmTDjAJ
146. https://www.vedantu.com/revision-notes/cbse-class-6-science-notes-chapter-5
147. https://nps.cmr.ac.in/blog/studentblogger-empathy-class-assembly-by-aisiri-girish-grade-12g-cmrnps/
148. https://positivepsychology.com/kindness-activities-empathy-worksheets/
149. https://www.youtube.com/watch?v=Itp21tly8nM
150. https://www.cbse.gov.in/cbsenew/list-of-manuals/life_skills_cce.pdf
151. https://www.cbse.gov.in/cbsenew/documents/Handbook%20for%20Teachers.pdf
152. https://cbseacademic.nic.in/web_material/ValueEdu/Value%20Education%20Kits.pdf
153. https://cmrgandhipublicschool.com/cultivating-empathy-and-open-mindedness-among-students/
154. https://crispindia.net/assets/files/Publication/Study/Class%2010_Bio_Structured%20LP%20Book.pdf
155. https://www.niu.edu/citl/resources/guides/instructional-guide/rubrics-for-assessment.shtml
156. https://citl.indiana.edu/teaching-resources/assessing-student-learning/rubric-creation-use/index.html#:~:text=A%20rubric%20is%20a%20tool,average%20performance%20for%20each%20trait.

157. https://theartofeducation.edu/2017/03/ceramics-scaffolding-curriculum-example/
158. https://thepotterywheel.com/how-to-make-pottery-at-home/
159. https://www.instagram.com/reel/C7wpDizAzvo/
160. https://www.edutopia.org/blog/scaffolding-lessons-six-strategies-rebecca-alber?qt-edu_blogs_popular_sidebar=1
161. https://theartofeducation.edu/2015/10/visually-scaffold-your-curriculum-with-ease/
162. https://www.youtube.com/watch?v=7gl3PogKfuA
163. https://wheelandclay.com/blog/slab-building-lesson-plan/
164. https://eyfs.info/articles.html/teaching-and-learning/creative-diaries-clay-work-in-the-early-years-r203/
165. https://byjus.com/biology/flower/
166. https://www.vedantu.com/biology/flower
167. https://www.trees.com/gardening-and-landscaping/flowers
168. https://www.youtube.com/watch?v=A4YIpGQiD3w
169. https://study.com/academy/lesson/insect-pollination-process-diagram-adaptations.html
170. https://byjus.com/english/flower-names/
171. https://creeperplants.com/all-season-flowering-plants/
172. https://www.scribd.com/document/372705880/grade-6

173. https://study.com/academy/lesson/style-of-a-flower-function-lesson-quiz.html
174. https://byjus.com/ncert-solutions/ncert-solutions-class-4-evs-chapter-5-anita-and-the-honeybees/
175. https://www.fondriest.com/news/the-birds-and-the-bees-understanding-the-diversity-of-pollinators.htm
176. https://www.ugaoo.com/blogs/ornamental-gardening/summer-flowers-in-india-seasonal-flowers
177. https://www.vedantu.com/evs/flowering-plants-names
178. https://www.embibe.com/exams/parts-of-a-flower/
179. https://flexbooks.ck12.org/cbook/ck-12-cbse-science-class-6/section/4.5/primary/lesson/flower-and-its-parts/
180. https://primaryleap.co.uk/activity/parts-of-a-flower
181. https://www.amnh.org/learn-teach/curriculum-collections/biodiversity-counts/plant-identification/plant-morphology/parts-of-a-flower
182. https://flexbooks.ck12.org/cbook/ck-12-cbse-biology-class-11/section/5.7/primary/lesson/the-flower/
183. https://www.crestolympiads.com/topic/class-3-parts-of-a-plant
184. https://www.embibe.com/questions/Mention-the-function-of-the-flower./EM2570586
185. https://www.doubtnut.com/pcmb-questions/55763
186. https://byjus.com/cbse-notes/cbse-class-6-science-notes-chapter-7-getting-to-know-plants/

187. https://www.vedantu.com/revision-notes/cbse-class-4-evs-notes-chapter-5-anita-and-the-honeybees
188. https://ncert.nic.in/textbook/pdf/deap105.pdf
189. https://ncert.nic.in/textbook/pdf/desa101.pdf
190. https://www.usgs.gov/faqs/why-are-pollinating-bats-birds-bees-butterflies-and-other-animals-important
191. https://www.youtube.com/watch?v=BfYXNe4BBxE
192. https://www.vedantu.com/question-answer/mean-by-seasonal-plants-describe-any-five-class-11-biology-cbse-5fd79cbac0af9500a2b94c8d
193. https://www.youtube.com/watch?v=j9YSOrjoRFk
194. https://mahindranursery.com/blogs/plant-guide/seasonal-flowers-in-india-%F0%9F%8C%B8-year-round-guide-to-beautiful-blooms-by-mahindra-nursery-exports
195. https://www.successcds.net/learn-english/class-9/important-questions/moments-book-chapter-1-the-lost-child
196. https://www.drishtiias.com/images/pdf/science%20class%206.pdf
197. https://www.interflora.in/blog/gardening-for-kids-easy-flowers-to-grow
198. https://cbseacademic.nic.in/web_material/Curriculum/Vocational/2018/HORTICULTURE%20XI%20(816)/Floriculture%20-I%20XI.pdf

199. https://www.eurokidsindia.com/blog/discover-common-flower-names-for-kids.php
200. https://www.dezeen.com/2024/03/30/nest-shaped-buildings-roundups/
201. https://theconstructor.org/architecture/principles-of-biophilic-design/564602/
202. https://www.re-thinkingthefuture.com/articles/use-of-natural-materials-in-architecture-design/
203. https://materialdistrict.com/article/how-mud-could-revolutionise-building-materials-and-lower-costs/
204. https://thursd.com/articles/davide-macullo-architects-the-leaves-albania
205. https://energy.mit.edu/news/using-natures-structures-in-wooden-buildings/
206. https://www.re-thinkingthefuture.com/articles/biomimicry-as-a-concept-of-architecture/
207. https://www.linkedin.com/advice/1/how-can-you-incorporate-natural-materials-your-architectural-4q9cf
208. https://houses-apartments.com/en/architecture/architecture-interplay/how-does-architecture-interplay-affect-the-use-of-natural-materials-in-building-design
209. https://www.re-thinkingthefuture.com/articles/using-the-five-elements-of-nature-in-architecture/
210. https://www.re-thinkingthefuture.com/designing-for-typologies/a13346-designing-with-nature-in-mind/
211. https://en.wikipedia.org/wiki/Twig_work

212. https://architecturecompetitions.com/architecture-projects/lattice-structure-crafted-from-natural-twigs-and-steel-integrates-seamlessly-with-ecological-bird-watching-environment
213. https://www.pinterest.com/ideas/building-with-branches/909352682032/
214. https://www.pinterest.com/debster456/sticks-branches-and-twigs-oh-my/
215. https://www.asiarchitectural.com/how-connection-to-nature-is-driving-the-next-generation-of-architects/
216. https://www.modlar.com/news/396/the-art-of-blending-architecture-with-natural-surroundings/
217. https://www.sciencedirect.com/science/article/pii/S2095263514000363
218. https://www.architectmagazine.com/design/wall-fitting-revisited-a-study-in-organic-architecture_o
219. https://americancablerigging.com/how-cable-rigging-products-are-used-in-architecture/
220. https://thefloodhub.co.uk/wp-content/uploads/2025/02/FT-Q-C40-Lesson-3-Lesson-Plan-Teachers-Notes.pdf
221. https://teacherbot.io/contents/create-a-lesson-plan-for-primary-6-children-on-rivers-flowing-down-to-
222. https://www.youtube.com/watch?v=thAHwm1rdUw
223. https://www.vedantu.com/revision-notes/cbse-class-4-evs-notes-chapter-13-a-rivers-tale

224. https://www.theedadvocate.org/teaching-students-about-the-causes-and-effects-of-water-pollution/
225. https://byjus.com/cbse/class-4-science-syllabus/
226. https://www.scribd.com/document/738931245/CB-SE-Syllabus-Class-4-EVS-1
227. https://oercommons.org/courseware/lesson/90432/overview
228. https://fr.scribd.com/document/632910079/Rivers-Livelihood-Lesson-Plan
229. https://thefloodhub.co.uk/ks2-lesson-3/
230. https://www.ncert.nic.in/pdf/syllabus/08Environmental%20(III-V).pdf
231. https://www.extramarks.com/studymaterials/cbse/cbse-class-5-evs-syllabus/
232. https://www.rgs.org/schools/resources-for-schools/rivers
233. https://byjus.com/cbse-notes/class-7-social-science-geography-chapter-5-water/
234. https://water.dpie.nsw.gov.au/__data/assets/pdf_file/0006/546621/module-three-lesson-plan.pdf
235. https://www.vedantu.com/content-files-downloadable/revision-notes/cbse-class-4-evs-notes-chapter-13-a-rivers-tale.pdf
236. https://aifacilitator.community/lesson-plans/class-7/SST/7.10%20Our%20Environment%20-%20Our%20Changing%20Earth.pdf

237. https://www.dorsetcoast.com/wp-content/uploads/2024/09/DORSET-Lesson-3-Lesson-Plan-Teachers-Notes-1.pdf
238. https://www.wwf.org.uk/sites/default/files/2020-04/WWF_RiverStory_Educator_Pack.pdf

Image Copyright Information

1. **Pat Morita who played Mr. Miyagi:** Kingkongphoto & www.celebrity-photos.com from Laurel Maryland, USA, CC BY-SA 2.0 <https://creativecommons.org/licenses/by-sa/2.0>, via Wikimedia Commons
2. **Dino Game:** Blaka suta/Shutterstock.com
3. **Report Card:** pexelsstock/Shutterstock.com
4. **Tintin:** River Cruise Mentor/Shutterstock.com
5. **Tintin 2:** Erman Gunes/Shutterstock.com
6. **Tintin 3:** Ferran Cornellà, CC BY-SA 3.0 <https://creativecommons.org/licenses/by-sa/3.0>, via Wikimedia Commons
7. **Pigeon:** NICKY1841/Shutterstock.com
8. **Vulture:** Kike.garcia.85/Shutterstock.com
9. **Stephen Hawking:** Koca Vehbi/Shutterstock.com
10. **Farming 1:** William Edge/Shutterstock.com
11. **Farming 2:** Viktor Sergeevich/Shutterstock.com
12. **Greta Thunberg:** Daniele COSSU/Shutterstock.com
13. **Jiddu Krishnamurti:** Public domain, via Wikimedia Commons
14. **Water Wheel:** Steve Travelguide/Shutterstock.com
15. **Iraq's Water Crisis:** Sebastian Castelier/Shutterstock.com

16. **Mumbai:** Julia Bond/Shutterstock.com
17. **Mumbai skyscraper:** balajisrinivasan/Shutterstock.com
18. **Anne Frank:** Unknown photographer, Public domain, via Wikimedia Commons
19. **Bird released from cage** – Black Creator 24/Shutterstock.com
20. **Stack of Magnetic Balls** – MY10/Shutterstock.com
21. **Threads and Yarn** – Neliakott/Shutterstock.com
22. **Marble Balls** – Apostle/Shutterstock.com
23. **Picture of Writer's Daughter:** Credit due to Tania Ghosh
24. **Lost my Keys:** Andrey_Popov/Shutterstock.com
25. **Picnic:** oneinchpunch/Shutterstock.com
26. **Curriculum Vitae:** Kittisophon/Shutterstock.com
27. **Carbon Di Oxide:** Meggi/Shutterstock.com
28. **Water Molecule:** struna/Shutterstock.com
29. **Child learning Technology:** Cherdchai101/Shutterstock.com
30. **Bicycle:** arturnichiporenko/Shutterstock.com
31. **Tree:** Pornsawan Baipakdee/Shutterstock.com
32. **Water Cycle:** Amado Designs/Shutterstock.com